Modern Soviet Society

GORBACHEV'S
RUSSIA

BASILE KERBLAY

TRANSLATED BY RUPERT SWYER

PANTHEON BOOKS
NEW YORK

LIBRARY OF CONGRESS CATALOGING-IN-PUBLICATION DATA
Kerblay, Basile H.
  Gorbachev's Russia / by Basile Kerblay.
      p.   cm.
  Bibliography: p.
  Includes index.
  ISBN 0-394-75971-0
  1. Soviet Union—Social conditions—1970-
2. Soviet Union—Politics and government—1982-   I. Title.
HN523.5.K395   1989
947.085'4—dc19   88-28573

Book Design by Ann Gold
Manufactured in the United States of America

First Edition

Contents

PREFACE

■ To some people the publication of a new book about the Soviet Union while Mikhail Gorbachev's reforms are in progress is bound to seem naïve, while others will view the undertaking as rash. It will seem naïve to those who assume from the outset that the initiatives of the general secretary of the Communist Party are simply the kind of fine promises all new governments make; to others, it simply seems too risky to try to pronounce upon a situation that is complex, shifting, and inchoate.

I do believe it is possible to make a useful contribution to the discussion of trends in the Soviet Union, however, by standing aside from the conventional views. Sovietologists generally focus on the political regime or the workings of the economy; they give pride of place to scenarios of conflict and change in the leadership or analyse economic performance, but they cast only an occasional glance at society, for the well-bred scholar holds that society has no leverage on so rigid a system. I believe, on the contrary, that it is in the changes taking place in society that we should seek the roots of the problems currently facing the country's leaders, and there that we should assess the likelihood of success for the reforms that have been brought forward to tackle them. In other words, I am concerned primarily with the capacity for change of the main strata of Soviet society and with the processes that these reforms are likely to set in train at some time in the future.

Another feature of my approach is my concern with longer-term trends. It is not within the historian's power to assess the effectiveness of a policy until enough time has elapsed to enable him to appreciate its results. On the other hand, he does have a duty to try to place events in a broader perspective than the journalist's, who is mainly concerned with current events. The reforms now in progress and debates surrounding them should not mislead us into thinking that they have sprung up spontaneously, at a wave of Gorbachev's magic wand.

I have begun this study with a reminder of the origins of the economic and social problems that have arisen over the past thirty years, as a result of discordances between social structures, political institutions, and cultural aspirations. This is not the first time since Stalin's death in 1953 that attempts have been made to provide a remedy. Thanks to glasnost, people now feel freer to express themselves, and currents of thought already seen in the 1960s, regarding the need for decentralization, greater autonomy for enterprises, the need to bring legality into public life, are surfacing once more; Gorbachev is offering them what could prove to be their last chance of prevailing.

What is Gorbachev trying to achieve?

We are all familiar with the watchwords of his reform campaign: transparency or openness (glasnost), restructuring (perestroika), and democracy. However, we should not take this last term in the sense ascribed to it in the Western democracies. The misunderstanding does not lie in the intentions of the leadership, which has consistently stressed that it is not its intention to introduce a market economy or a representative pluralist regime, but to give the economy a shot in the arm by encouraging initiative and efficiency, and by stimulating more active involvement by the population in all spheres of public life. The Party has no intention of relinquishing either its ideological monopoly or its control over all aspects of social life.

That raises the question of whether this policy is not hamstrung by structural inconsistency from the outset. How does one reconcile autonomy for enterprises with the preservation of central planning to lay down guidelines, state orders, and certain essential prices? How can freedom of contractual relations be assured when enterprises are in a monopoly position vis-à-vis each other?

What can Gorbachev do about this? Is Soviet society capable of accepting change? Is there not a risk that the new calls for efficiency may go unheeded because the prime motive force – the spirit of enterprise – is sadly lacking? Collectivization destroyed the bedrock of traditional society, which was the community, and atomized the population. How can one mobilize it for renewed effort without immediately giving something in return, when the groups that make up civil society in other countries (labour unions, associations, churches, etc.) are here the direct offshoots of the Party, or else under its control? Further, the population has grown individualist in its behaviour, even if it does retain some of the reflexes of its peasant roots, such as hostility to inequality and personal wealth. Here, as elsewhere, rigid attitudes are the chief obstacle to change.

We ought not, however, to underestimate the dynamic that glasnost has set in motion. Its effects are bound to make themselves felt in the fairly near future, making a reversion to the status quo ante highly unlikely.

The first of these consequences is the emergence of public opinion, which is visible in the eagerness with which people devour newspapers and follow TV discussions, and even more so in the influence that certain movements are coming to exert in sensitive areas such as ecology, the preservation of the national heritage, and the building of nuclear power stations, to the point where they are starting to affect decisions. Most such campaigns have been sparked by the intelligentsia in the press and have been taken up by the young, who are highly sensitive to everything affecting the environment, besides being influenced by certain Western fashions, in reaction to established dogma in their own country.

The second effect of glasnost has grown out of the condemnation of Stalinism, which has led to a search for legitimacy in the teachings of Lenin, in the rehabilitation of the victims of the purges of the 1930s, and in the revival of the intellectual and political debates of the 1920s. The intelligentsia has taken advantage of the opening to come out and raise the problem of morality in public life. These calls for an awakening of moral consciousness or a return to traditional – or even reactionary, in the case of the association called Pamyat – values could serve to catalyze mass movements in the event of economic or national crisis. Consequently, I have dwelt at some length on discussions such as those concerning the preservation of national languages and cultures under threat from modernization or Russification; although these problems are first aired by certain sections of the intelligentsia, they touch upon the shared aspirations and concerns of a much wider public.

The key test for the future will be the attitude of the population once economic reforms start to bite. I have therefore tried to consider the prospects for price reform and redundancies in certain sectors of the economy. Surely there is a risk that threats to purchasing power and job security could undermine the social pact that has been the basis of working-class acceptance of the Soviet regime and labour-union compliance.

Some readers may be surprised that I have said nothing

about the right attitude to adopt toward present trends in the Soviet Union.

I have tried to remain as objective as possible, and this aim has precluded any value judgements concerning events now unfolding, whose full implications are by no means clear as yet. Moreover, two implicit convictions have shaped my attitude. The first is that politics is not just a matter of technical choices, and that such decisions must have a moral underpinning. Yet moral law is neither Christian, nor Jewish, nor Marxist: it is universal or it is nothing. To seek to divide up humanity in terms of the terrible memories of the past, or of outdated ideologies, or of shortsighted national interests, will be of little use in solving problems common to all countries: how to secure peace, how to permit the free movement of people and ideas, how to ensure growth and full employment, and how to eradicate poverty.

But we must not confuse political decision-making with morality. Policies must take account of what is possible, not only what is desirable, so compromise is the result. Individual morality has no room for compromise; if it did, no act could be truly moral. As an individual, I am free to adopt an attitude of nonviolence when dealing with an adversary, but a political leader cannot force a nation to act altruistically; he must take individuals as they are. That indeed is the conclusion reached by foreign leaders after their talks with Gorbachev: regardless their differences, they all credit him with a desire for change and openness. Such trust is the sole basis for genuine international security, though the policies must be judged by their results. But to prejudge these results and allow the potential adversary to become mired in his difficulties would merely fuel the vicious spiral that leads from a sense of weakness to fear, and from fear to aggression.

What is more, efforts to influence the Soviet regime from outside – notably, with embargoes – have always ended in failure, because there is no way in which outside pressures can exert leverage on the regime. On the contrary, the internal situation of the USSR and the portion of Europe under its control determine the potential scope for opening up and an easing of tensions. Unfortunately, perestroika provides no immediate answer to the difficulties of every-day life or to the most acute of the country's chronic problems, such as blasé youth, which could one day erupt into protest, or the more unpredictable and emotionally charged problems relating to certain nationalities.

Moreover, restructuring can only succeed if it does not create disturbances in neighboring countries – if that hap-pens, advocates of the Brezhnev doctrine will waste little time intervening. This explains why Gorbachev is urging his allies to follow his example and ease domestic tensions as much as possible. All that adds up to a great many unknowns for a policy which, like any far-reaching change, will take years to bear fruit.

The Russian has shown me in so many instances how even an enslavement and an oppression that continually overwhelm all powers of resistance need not necessarily bring about a degeneration of the soul. There exists, at least in the soul of the Slav, a degree of submission which deserves the epithet perfect, because even under the most massive and annihilating pressure it creates for the soul a secret arena, a fourth dimension in which, however grievous conditions become, a new endless and genuinely independent freedom can now begin.

— Rainer Maria Rilke, Letter to Major-General von Sedlakowitz, December 9, 1920

GORBACHEV'S RUSSIA

1

■

NEW TRENDS IN SOVIET SOCIETY

■

■ It is never easy to describe the direction a society is taking, because its future is never predetermined. The history of the USSR in particular serves as a constant reminder of what it owes to one or another of its leaders, who, for better or worse, have altered the course of events. Among those leaders, Mikhail Gorbachev will unquestionably represent a decisive step forward in the history of the Soviet Union, even though it is not always easy to distinguish words and intentions from actual deeds, or what is happening in Moscow or Leningrad from everyday conditions in the provinces.[1] But the task is further complicated by the need, after analysing the various mechanisms of Soviet society, to develop a comprehensive view of how they interact.

THE COMPONENTS OF THE SYSTEM: CONTINUITY AND CHANGE

Comprehensive models that seek to define the system generally start by focusing on either the economy or ideology as the determining factor in other spheres. Soviet doctrine draws its inspiration from the Marxist teaching that control of the means of production and exchange by the state is sufficient to radically modify the structure of social relations; this accounts for the disproportionate importance accorded to the economy in the concerns of the nation's leaders. According to this interpretation, the Bolshevik Revolution should be regarded as the inevitable outcome of the growth of nineteenth-century Russian industry and capitalism; Stalinism, therefore, was rendered necessary by faster industrialization in the 1930s, while today the maturity and complexity of the industrial system call for the type of reform that has been set in motion to boost efficiency.

Sovietologists, who base their analysis on the specific characteristics of Soviet ideology and power, argue that the October Revolution predates the country's economic development. Bringing the means of production under state control does not in itself create wealth: it consolidates the power of the regime. Power is the key factor, whereas plans are subject to constant review. In this view, the ultimate driving force behind the development of the system is to be sought in ideology and the circulation of the political elites. As long as ideology remains unchanged, we have grounds for doubting the system's capacity for change.

My own analysis rejects the vision of a monolithic, changeless Soviet system. Each of its three essential components – power, society, and culture – develops along its own, unsynchronized, lines. Each of these three variables has a dynamic of its own. It is important to bear this in mind, because it is from the discordance between them that the tensions or problems facing the Soviets today arise.

Of the three spheres, the political system is the most stable. A mere nine leaders have run the country since 1917. Their power still rests upon four pillars, none of which has ever been challenged, even in the current period:

- The leading role of the Party, a principle that rules out any kind of pluralism.
- Social ownership of the means of production, which gives to the leadership absolute control over production, jobs, and pay.
- Democratic centralism, which allows the central authorities to appoint officials at all levels of the hierarchy (*nomenklatura*) and to integrate a composite society to form a single whole.
- The monopoly of education and information, and the censorship that is its corollary.

Within this rigid framework, however, we may observe a certain number of trends affecting the composition of the Party, the influence of the bureaucracy, and the significance of ideology.

According to Lenin and the intellectuals who formed the majority of his machine, the Party was originally meant to be a revolutionary group whose membership was confined to an elite. From 1926 on, however, it was submerged by a wave of militants recruited to take over the administration of the country. These newcomers, hastily trained in the people's universities (*rabfaks*), were of humble origins, and their style of command and narrow-mindedness remain a feature of many of the country's managers and officials. A new generation of officials of middle-class origin, trained in the higher engineering colleges and the universities, has arisen since World War II, and is tending to take over from its predecessors. The gap between the two types of political and economic manager is particularly evident today.

The leadership and supervisory functions that the Party has taken upon itself are what legitimize this flood of specialists into the apparatus; this is reflected even in the membership of the Central Committee, which numbers only twenty or so workers and peasants out of a total of

453. One result of the professionalization of the Party cadres and the incorporation of the technical elites has been to substitute rational criteria, based on expert recommendations, for the earlier voluntarist decision-making. Moreover, this category of personnel has sought to stabilize its position and consolidate its privileges by strengthening legal procedures and review channels, in order to protect itself from arbitrary decisions. Consequently, membership in the establishment has become a stable social status, which can be transmitted to one's descendants, notably by means of the prestigious schools reserved to the children of the elite.

Regardless of generation, the apparatchik retains a preference for democratic centralism, under which he must seek approval from higher authority for decisions for which he does not wish to shoulder responsibility himself. To that should be added the logic of a command economy, which has spawned a cumbersome hierarchy of state committees (Gosplan, Gossnab, etc.), technical ministries at federal and republic levels, unions of industrial or agro-industrial enterprises, and so forth, each having its own regulatory powers. This proliferating bureaucracy cancels out the theoretical advantages that might be expected from a planned economy, especially in a period of perpetual technological change.

Ideology in turn, with its nineteenth-century dogmas, is incapable of producing practical political solutions. The economic choices and external relations of the USSR are not subject to any predetermined rules. The ideology that inspired the early decisions of the Bolshevik Revolution is now no more than a source of legitimation of the regime. It posits that the state is led by a moral elite inspired by a scientific doctrine that confers quasi-religious infallibility upon it. Ideology has become debased to the level of a stereotyped discourse that no longer has any bearing on reality.[2] This means that science and technology are beyond its control and that spheres of intellectual autonomy have emerged independently of its wishes, from which the world of arts and letters would like to benefit as well.

Ideology does still enjoy the privilege of supplying all citizens, from infancy onward, with a common political culture based on a handful of intangible postulates – e.g. job security, full employment, the condemnation of personal profit – which create an illusory surface conformism, behind which a society made up of many different social strata has grown up, fashioned by the transformations common to all industrial civilizations.

The modernization of society did not begin with the new regime, but it has been hastened by its methods. Urban growth in the wake of industrialization has profoundly altered the nature of Soviet society, which ceased to be predominantly rural more than a quarter of a century ago.[3] Almost 40 per cent of the population is now concentrated in towns of more than 100,000 inhabitants. The sizable movement from the countryside to the towns – one engineer in two in Leningrad was not born in that city[4] – has radically altered people's lifestyles: housing conditions, the status of women, education for children, leisure. This flight from the villages and the land has reached alarming proportions in certain regions, such as Russia's non-black lands, and the policy of amalgamating villages has often merely accelerated the exodus.

Among the changes that are most decisive for the future, women's new perceptions of their role, under the impact of education and salaried employment, is engendering a series of demographic and sociological phenomena. Already, fertility in Russia is just sufficient to maintain the same level of population (the population of the USSR as a whole is growing, but solely as a result of high fertility rates in the predominantly rural republics of Central Asia). The authoritarian model inherited from rural tradition, which conferred upon the father the role of leader, in the image of the sovereign – cf. the 'little father of the peoples' – is rejected today. The resulting crisis of authority in the family is evidenced in the high divorce rate, in single-parent families, and in disoriented youth, who are more attentive to the influence of the street than to the urgings of the older generations.

Even so, the traditional behavioural models retain their hold, both in the unequal distribution of tasks in the husband's favour inside the family and in the workings of the institutions.[5] It is not uncommon, particularly in outlying regions, for senior officials to run the region, factory, kolkhoz, institute, or theatre, as their personal property, thus perpetuating the servile attitudes of their subordinates.[6]

The growth of the towns has facilitated schooling and led to steadily rising educational standards, which have in turn altered the scale of values. Now that 60 per cent of a given age group receives full secondary education (ten years of schooling), competition for admission to higher education and for good jobs has become increasingly fierce. A candidate's social background often counts for more than his merit. Young people greatly resent these inequalities. With their scientific training, moreover, they are less and less ready to put up with a system whose irrationality contradicts the principles on which it claims to be based.

Here, as elsewhere, universal schooling and the development of audio-visual techniques have greatly enhanced the impact of the mass media in the Soviet Union. Public speakers are no longer in direct touch with their public, and, to be credible, they need to adapt their language to what the listener or the viewer expects to hear. Thus a new style of communications has emerged, one that will only become fully meaningful as time goes on. Furthermore, the intrusion into the Soviet world of foreign models, through tourism, co-operation agreements, and foreign radio stations, are helping to open up the intellectual horizons of population to outside influences.[7] These in turn are jostling received ideas and stimulating new needs.

In the cultural sphere, modernization has contributed to the secularization of society and the erosion of traditional cultures. Consumer behaviour is growing more uniform, and material objects now serve as a means of cultural identification for members of a particular section of society, such as rugs and chandeliers for the 'petty bourgeois' or audio equipment for young, well-off citydwellers. But mass culture and consumer values do not affect all regions and all age groups in the same way. A recent film by Nikita Mikhalkov illustrates the contrast between a young rock fan and his grandmother, who has come to visit him in the city and still hews to the traditional values. The values vary from one nationality to another, but everywhere the sense of family obligations remains foremost, such as modesty in women and honour in men. These may stretch to acts of vengeance and nepotism in the remoter regions of the union. There, ties of kinship are as strong as ever, being admirably suited to the requirements of the parallel market in everyday life and to overcoming the barriers to admission to certain schools, hospitals, institutes, etc.

Russification primarily affects the minor nationalities, as they have little by little lost the use of their language.[8] On the other hand, the bilingualism of the non-Russian nationalities is not felt to be a threat as long as schools that teach in the indigenous language remain open.[9] The development of Soviet education has promoted native elites to functions in which they serve as intermediaries between mass culture and the culture of their people. Paradoxically, it is the marginal group that has most fully assimilated Soviet civilization, the intelligentsia, that nowadays gives expression to the national consciousness of the minorities. As in other multinational countries, the standardization of lifestyles and the disappearance of the old communities are leading the uprooted individual to seek an identity in the nationality of parents and grandparents, or in the national religion.[10]

Meanwhile, the humanist tradition, which is still present

via the great classics of Russian literature, continues to provide sustenance to the elite of the intelligentsia, preserving a sense of universal values able to satisfy the demands of the spirit, awaiting only the green light from the authorities to come out into the open, as is happening today. Bolder spirits, unable to bide their time, were imprisoned or exiled, so that dissidence has not played much of a role in recent developments. The cultural sphere has not succeeded in winning autonomy; but then neither have the authorities succeeded in bringing forth a new Soviet man from the profusion of legacies of the past.

STRUCTURAL STRAINS AND ATTEMPTS AT ADJUSTMENT

Thus the respective dynamics of the political, societal, and cultural spheres are not synchronized. This gives rise to discordances that Soviet sociologists have finally acknowledged, although they point out that the contradictions are not antagonistic. We shall confine ourselves to noting the most obvious among them:

- In the economic sphere, centralism and bureaucratic inertia are a brake on the dynamism that the leadership is calling for, even though the workers put up with it perfectly well, unaware that slower growth hinders social mobility.
- In the political sphere, the Party's grip in every area, in its disregard for any separation of powers, has a sterilizing effect on initiative, while the elimination of civil society renders citizens apolitical and passive, and stifles national cultures beneath an appearance of federalism.[11]
- In the cultural sphere, the official ideology is losing all credibility among the masses, who contrast the higher morality of the 'builders of communism' with present-

day behaviour, and among the elites, whose stringent rationalism has no time for placing history on a pedestal or for doublethink.

These incompatibilities between structures and behaviour create strains, but they have not paralyzed the system. First, because some of the regime's values coincide with the communal tradition of peasant societies, based on mutual help, equality, respect for authority, and the exclusion of nonconformists. 'Socialism' provides job security for all, and satisfaction of elementary basic needs such as subsistence, housing, education, and welfare; these are the priorities of the great majority of citizens. The frustration people feel in this respect due to shortages, lack of social amenities, and social inequalities do not preclude a broad consensus on the aims of the present regime, insofar as a foreigner is able to judge as he peers beneath the conformist exterior of the Soviet people.

On the other hand, individuals have displayed considerable ingenuity in adapting to the system's shortcomings by inventing compensating circuits to make good the inadequacies of the legal channels. As a result, an increasingly flourishing parallel economy has arisen to overcome the lack of goods and services. It would be impossible to enumerate the range of markets that exists, from the legal kolkhozian market for produce grown on the family farms, to the black market for books, theatre tickets, sporting events, imported goods (*fartsovshchiki*), via under-the-counter deals between factories on a 'you scratch my back, I'll scratch yours' basis. Everyone gets by, has his 'arrangements,' to illustrate that familiar Soviet joke: 'The stores are empty, but everyone's got what he needs at home.' An estimated 17–18 million people are engaged, full-time or part-time, in some kind of parallel activity (repairs, private medicine, tutoring, etc.) in addition to their regular job or after retirement. For a much smaller public, similarly, there has grown up a parallel culture, in the shadow of the official censorship, in which writers, artists, and musicians can express themselves within a narrow circle of friends or through limited samizdat editions.

These spontaneous forms of adjustment to the system's shortcomings are hugely wasteful of resources[12] and human energy, breeding inequality and resentment prejudicial to the social climate.[13] They are mere palliatives; more radical solutions could come only from above.

Various partial reforms have been attempted since the death of Stalin in 1953, with a view to 'perfecting' the existing system. Nikita Khrushchev was the first to initiate (often hasty) moves on all fronts. His revelations of Stalin's crimes in February 1956 – a first glimmer of glasnost – were reserved for Party members. In the process of de-Stalinization, the literary 'thaw' spurred a short-lived literary renaissance from 1956 to 1962.[14] His attempts at decentralizing the administration of the economy by setting up regional economic councils (*sovnarkhoz*) in place of certain ministries, in 1957, whetted local appetites (*mestnichestvo*) and ended in failure. All that has survived of his reforms is the abolition of the tractor stations and the repeal, in 1956, of the wartime laws that mobilized labour at its place of work (abandoning one's post used to be punished severely). Free movement of labour was a serious blow to the coherence of the system, because thereafter the work force acquired a degree of autonomy comparable to that of a market economy – aside from the fact that the state is the sole employer. Enterprises now had to compete for labour; shrewd workers and managers turned the situation to advantage to secure more relaxed discipline and unwarranted bonuses through overtime, where they could not obtain better working conditions.[15] But when Khrushchev tried to reform the Party organization, the Party turned and ousted him in 1964.

Leonid Brezhnev, as Party secretary in 1964–72, followed the opposite tack: he re-established the sectoral ministries and condemned dissident writers. As a fillip to the economy, enterprises were given some freedom (e.g., the 1965 reform inspired by Lieberman's proposals), but the centralized methods soon resumed as enterprises were grouped into 'unions', as if sheer size could make up for lack of worker motivation and poorly trained managers.[16] Whereas Khrushchev had made the Party machine nervous, Brezhnev sought on the contrary to allay its fears, considerably slowing the replacement of Party cadres.[17] After eighteen years of stability, the Party machine had grown old and economic growth slower, which explains why that period is now referred to as the 'years of stagnation' (zastoinye gody).

On balance, the overall picture is not all that negative, when one considers that Brezhnev's Soviet Union achieved arms parity, which provided a basis for temporary détente with the United States,[18] or when one considers the development of energy resources in Siberia to pay for technology transfers. The policy of legalization has been pursued through the publication of 158 fundamental laws and a revision of the 1977 Constitution. The Politburo has come to act as the arbiter between the different state organizations represented within it, although there are no signs of any stirrings of a plurality of interests, which would be incompatible with formal unanimity over objectives. The legalization of procedures for the transmission of power has enabled the three general secretaries since Brezhnev to achieve office without crisis or disruption.[19]

The most urgent problems faced by Brezhnev's successors were flagging growth, technological backwardness, corruption and favouritism in the administration, and slack discipline in the workplace, largely due to alcoholism, which has become a scourge of Soviet society. The economy was not going to pick up merely because of a change of leader. It was labouring under objective handicaps such as dwindling natural resources, rising costs for extracting ore in remote Siberia, and a shrinking pool of surplus labour.[20] What is more, cuts in military spending as a proportion of national income (currently more than 15 per cent) depend on the outcome of arms-control negotiations, which will have an even more decisive impact on future investment than on consumption. On the other hand, measures could be taken right away to strengthen discipline at work (without which the best techniques are worthless) and restore the image of the Party, tarnished by the petty corruption of so many of its members.

The choice of Yuri Andropov (12 November 1982 to 9 February 1984) to succeed Leonid Brezhnev, in place of the 'heir apparent', Chernenko, may be accounted for by this internal situation as well as by external conditions. Andropov had been ambassador to Budapest from 1954 to 1957, and director of relations with the socialist countries at the Secretariat of the Central Committee from 1962 to 1967, in which year he became head of the KGB. That is to say, he was better informed as to the true situation both inside his country and abroad.[21] As a member of the Politburo since 1973, he was aware of the extent of corruption and had knowledge of compromising incidents involving Party notables and even certain people close to Brezhnev.[22]

Trials of senior officials and a handful of prominent

THE SOVIET ECONOMY'S DWINDLING PERFORMANCE

	ANNUAL GNP GROWTH		AVERAGE CEREALS CROP
	Official Figures	*Estimates*[a]	*(In Millions of Metric Tons)*
1971–75	5.1	3.7	181.5
1976–80	3.8	2.7	205.0
1981–85	3.1	2.2	180.3

[a]Source: U.S. Congress, Joint Economic Committee.

black-marketeers affected only a small number of people and were approved by the public, which had suffered from their misdeeds.[23] Absenteeism, on the other hand, had become widespread and was causing substantial damage to the economy, reckoned in billions of working hours lost. Often enough the cause lay in shortages that obliged people to stand in line for hours outside stores, but it lay also in the habit of getting drunk on payday and at the end of each working day. To restore discipline in the factories, the authorities sought to generalize the organization of workers into autonomous teams or brigades, with wages to be paid, in proportion to each worker's contribution to the work of the group, from an overall contractual sum for a given objective. This gave foremen an incentive to weed out the goldbricks and drunkards. By the end of 1983, some 7 million of the 39 million workers in industry and construction were working and being paid on this basis.

The authorities also tried to curb alcohol consumption, which had rocketed from 7 litres of pure alcohol per inhabitant over the age of fourteen in 1950 to 14.6 litres in 1983,[24] by restricting business hours of places where alcohol is sold, and by raising the price of a bottle of vodka from 3.62 rubles to 8 rubles. This price hike was one of a series of retail price increases between 1978 and 1983 affecting gasoline, coffee, chocolate, furniture, rugs, furs, and so on, in an attempt to adjust for inflation. The ruble has lost more than half its value since 1960. The cost of living has doubled, rising at an annual rate of 3 per cent. Private savings accounts are swollen with surplus liquidity: 24 billion rubles were poured into these accounts in 1987, while retail sales rose by only 9.2 billion rubles.

The Polish crisis, which had been triggered by food price increases and gave birth to Solidarity, was still fresh in people's memories and served as a warning not to touch the price of foodstuffs. The state was thus forced to pay out heavy subsidies, given the real cost of farm produce. It also drove Andropov to keep up the repression of dissidents, which he had initiated when head of the KGB, until he had completely eliminated them from the political scene.

Meanwhile, far-reaching reforms had been undertaken in the economic, social, and political spheres, namely a reform of the enterprise, a modification of the educational system, and the rejuvenation of the Party apparatus. The full impact of these moves was to become clear only later.

After the trend to concentration of enterprises of the 1970s, the Soviet Union reverted, as in 1965, to the idea that the fate of production depended primarily on the margin of freedom and initiative the enterprises enjoyed. Accordingly, an experiment was launched in 1984 in which the enterprises of seven ministries were decentralized; this was to serve as a model for the restructuring of the whole of industry, enacted in 1987. We shall return to this act later on. In June 1983, 'workers' collectives' were established in all enterprises, as provided for under Article 8 of the Constitution. The assemblies of these collectives were invested with certain powers to control the appointment of managers, the application of the labour laws, the distribution of bonuses, housing, etc. Decisions, however, still remained in the hands of the management committees and were subject to the rules of democratic centralism. 'Self-management' here plainly does not mean what it means elsewhere. The law makes no provision for possible conflicts between the collective and management.

In April 1984, a law was enacted to reform all general schools in the educational system. This was justified by the need to improve vocational training for youth, to unify certain types of training in order to be able to award a diploma of secondary studies to all pupils after eleven years of schooling (instead of ten) from the age of six. On the other hand, the law cut the percentage of those going on to higher education: now almost 70 per cent of pupils completing the first cycle (Classes 1 to 8) are sent on to vocational schools (three years) or special technical schools (four years); only 25–30 per cent will be admitted to the second cycle (Classes 9 to 11), which leads to college. An additional effort was made for children from poor families (with a per capita income not exceeding 60 rubles), who will be exempted from payment for board, clothing, and school supplies. This affects children in rural areas particularly, who have to go to boarding schools in the towns due to the closing of many small village schools. The school reform had political goals, too – namely to reinforce the Marxist-Leninist convictions of young people and promote familiarity with the Russian language in the non-Russian republics, where Russian has been taught from kindergarten up since 1979. However, the Ministry of Higher Education's decision to make Russian compulsory in courses leading to the diploma of advanced studies had to be postponed and was not implemented until 1987. This was followed in 1988 by a complete overhaul of the educational system, inspired by recent moves to reduce bureaucratic supervision of teachers and encourage a sense of initiative in pupils.

The renewal of the Party machine began by weeding out the black sheep and went on from there, retiring those who had grown old under Brezhnev's long reign. Pending rejuvenation of the Central Committee by the twenty-seventh Party congress in 1986, new men such as Geydar Aliyev and Mikhail Solomentsev were brought into the Politburo as full members in 1983, and Vitaly Vorotnikov as a candidate member. Nikolai Ryzhkov was appointed to the Secretariat in November 1982, while Grigory Romanov and Yegor Ligachev joined it in 1983. When Andropov died, the 'Party [called] for a young and innovative leader'.[25] Instead, against all expectation, it got Chernenko, seventy-two, despite the fact that he was sick. He had been in charge of general affairs at the Secretariat from 1962 to 1976, and that had earned him the gratitude of all who owed their careers to him.

GORBACHEV AND HIS TEAM

In fact, the acting leader during Andropov's illness, and then under Chernenko, was Mikhail Gorbachev, as the man in charge of cadres in the Secretariat. His appointment as general secretary on 11 March 1985, following the death of the incumbent, came as no surprise even though he was not the only candidate for the post. Andrei Gromyko was the doyen of the Politburo, but his career outside the country had deprived him of a constituency inside the Party machine, unlike Grishin, first secretary of the Moscow Gorkom, or Romanov, who was backed by Leningrad. These two claimants were to be ousted from the Politburo, one in 1986, the other as early as 1985. Gromyko, on the other hand, delivered Gorbachev's investiture address and became president of the Supreme Soviet Presidium in July 1985, when Shevardnadze replaced him as foreign minister (a post Gromyko had held since 1957). Subsequent appointments and transfers to or within the Politburo and the Secretariat allowed Gorbachev to build his own team and strengthen his power.[26]

We know all too little about the circumstances and personal factors that enabled Gorbachev to rise so quickly through the hierarchy.[27] Though fairly young (fifty-four in 1985), he is not as young as all that: Khrushchev was fifty-nine in 1952, and Brezhnev fifty-eight in 1964. But his age places him at a pivotal point between two generations. As a child, he experienced the ordeals of collectivization, occupation, and the aftermath of the war. With his Moscow University education, he is as much at ease with the intelligentsia as with the peasants among whom he was born. From this background he draws his energy and practical sense, as well as an 'ability to get along with people different from himself'.[28] He seems to be a tolerant man; while he is not one to forget the past, he eschews putting people on trial for their former misdeeds.[29] His political experience began in the provincial city of Stavropol, as an aide to Kulakov, and Gorbachev later succeeded Fedor Kulakov in the Secretariat of the Central Committee, following the latter's death in 1978, as the Party's specialist on agricultural matters (he happens also to be a trained agronomist). His work has taken him abroad, to Canada, France, and Italy. Subsequently, in 1984, he visited Great Britain in his capacity as chairman of the Commission on Foreign Affairs of the Supreme Soviet, accompanied by his wife, Raisa. This journey confirmed his international stature and inaugurated a personal public-relations style before the world discovered the originality of his political position.

This originality lies less in his ideas, which he borrows frequently from his advisers, than in his courage and determination to press ahead with something more than a mere facelift in order to tackle the really deep-lying problems.

In the intellectual debate that has arisen in recent years, and in some cases much earlier, certain ideas have attracted particular attention.[30] Gorbachev's familiarity with the rural world has taught him more clearly than anyone else that the best spur to productivity is to give the worker a share in the profits. As far back as 1983, he gave the green light for the creation of autonomous work brigades, paid on the basis of what they harvested, in a large number of collective farms. Furthermore, in order to harness the potential of the family economy, the acreage allotted to families for private use ceased to be limited, provided their stock production was integrated with the collective production contract; for the first time in fifty years, horses made their appearance in the peasants' stables.[31] Collectivization has discovered the virtues of tenant farming.

In the industrial sphere, the institute responsible for this type of research at the Academy of Novosibirsk, which was run by Abel Aganbegyan, had arrived at similar conclusions, highlighting the importance of the 'human factor'

in the production system. Tatyana Zaslavskaya, who heads
the sociology section at this institute, had investigated
conflicts of interest generated by the way the Soviet economy operates, and in particular the resistance put up by
ministries to any kind of economic reform liable to curtail
their prerogatives or entail managerial responsibilities for
the managers. A confidential report written in April 1983
made this point and had reached the West,[32] where it
caused a sensation because it challenged a number of dogmas, such as the impossibility of antagonistic conflicts in
socialist society, and the virtues of bureaucratic centralism.
Zaslavskaya pointed out that the economic institutions inherited from the 1930s were out of touch with the technologies, level of education, and demands of the present-day
Soviet population; she argued that centralism paralyzed
creative initiative and informal activities within the sphere
of production and exchange, whereas these ought, on the
contrary, to be encouraged. In a word, the way forward out
of the economic maze lay through the study of the interests
of social groups.

Investigations along parallel lines had led D. Kurashvili
to condemn the shortcomings of the organization of the
economy into sectors, which had produced a compartmen-
talization of activities into a profusion of fiefs and ministries, at a time when, on the contrary, new technologies
were calling for co-operation across many different sectors.
He recommended a cut in the number of ministries by
giving intersectoral powers to a handful of state committees.[33] But the author harbored no illusions as to the fate
of his proposals, for a survey of members of the Central
Committee of the Georgian Party showed that only 18 per
cent favoured radical reform, while 36 per cent were for
the status quo.

So it has taken unflagging courage and great political
acumen for Gorbachev to swim against the current, tackling reforms whose chief characteristic has been to com-

bine economic measures (mostly along the lines of those already in effect since 1984 in certain industries) with far more spectacular departures in the political and social spheres, designed to encourage initiative and a sense of responsibility, starting with the Party. He has had to move energetically, but cautiously also, because any attempt to reform structures and attitudes is, by definition, a long-term task.

2

■

THE BROAD OUTLINES OF GORBACHEV'S POLICIES

■

■ Gorbachev's chief foreign-policy aims are to resume dialogue with the United States in order to achieve nuclear-arms cuts;[1] to pursue policies in Europe designed to foster neutralist tendencies in Germany, which is the cornerstone of the Western system; to secure an honourable, negotiated withdrawal from Afghanistan; and to clear up the dispute with China. On the home front, which is what we shall be discussing here, his main concern is the restructuring (perestroika) of the economic and social system in order to speed up (*uskorenie*) growth and 'democratize' the workings of the country's institutions, notably through greater willingness to accept criticism (glasnost).

GLASNOST AND THE ROLE OF THE MEDIA

The art of cultivating the media and the use of show-biz staging methods have long been part of the statesman's arsenal. Obviously, the leader of the Soviet Union is not subject to the same pressures as his counterpart in the United States, who needs to convince if his policies are to be credible. But here, as elsewhere, the obverse side of the medal is that the general public views politics as no more than a power struggle between clans.[2] Gorbachev has only to absent himself for a few weeks for the rumour mills to start rolling. Still, the personalization of politics engendered by his frequent TV appearances has served Gorbachev admirably. His charisma has stamped a new look on everything he does, contrasting with the official pomp of his predecessors.

The Soviet leadership possess considerable media striking power. The Agitprop, the propaganda section of the Central Committee, run by Alexander Yakovlev,[3] can call on an army of 4 million 'agitators', who are professional speakers trained in the Party schools or the universities of Marxism-Leninism, not to mention some 50,000 press, radio, and TV journalists turned out by the faculties of journalism – all members of the Party and thus duty-bound to advance its cause. But when they 'tried to present life through rose-colored glasses, the people saw through it all and gradually lost interest in the press'.[4] So the need arose to renew not only the style of the media, but their content as well.

The Russian word *glasnost* means 'to make known something that was previously concealed'. This has brought with it unprecedented disclosure of certain aspects of Soviet life, previously known to only a handful of specialists. Examples include the ravages of drugs and alcohol, prostitution, airplane accidents, natural disasters, an attempted hostage-taking, and the Chernobyl explosion. Soviet TV has inaugurated a new kind of broadcasting in which viewers are put directly in touch with foreigners, as in the hookup between Leningrad and Seattle, as well as with British and Japanese TV. The newspaper *Magnitogorskii rabochii* has published a series of articles by an American describing his impressions of his stay in Magnitogorsk. What is new is neither the printing of critical letters from readers – the Soviet press has always published those – nor the discussions carried on in the columns of *Literaturnaya Gazeta,* which had begun well before glasnost: the novelty is in the open attacks leveled at high-ranking officials, against the privileges of the *nomenklatura* or respected institutions such as the Academy of Sciences.[5] It is not just yesterday's leader who is being treated as a scapegoat, but the Party, through its corrupt members. Regional dignitaries who used to control the local press are liable to find themselves under attack from some journalist. They may take reprisals against the writer, but he knows now that he can count on support from the top, provided he is honest and does not go too far.[6]

The press's role as counterweight to those in power is admirably suited to the purposes of the 'cleanup' policy inaugurated in 1983, which is threatening all those cadres who are 'dragging their feet' in changing their style. 'The Party would not have succeeded,' Gorbachev acknowledges, 'had the media not played an active part.'[7] This in fact is a form of democracy envisaged by Nikolai Bukharin, who, as chief editor of *Pravda* in 1924, organized a network of correspondents in the countryside (*sel'kory*), to allow information to flow upward from the base to the summit independently of official channels.

Glasnost should not be construed as press freedom in the Western sense, in which public opinion is permitted to express itself on any topic outside officially authorized channels. Most of the criticisms published refer to the past or to everyday life; there has never been any discussion of Soviet foreign policy. The Soviet press does not exist to inform the public or please it, but to serve the priorities set by the Party plenums and denounce attitudes incompatible with those goals. As Gorbachev has said, 'Glasnost means criticism of shortcomings; it does not mean torpedoing socialism and its values.'[8]

Despite these limitations, glasnost has revived interest

in the press and in certain TV shows such as *The Twelfth Floor,* [9] in which political officials answer the public's questions directly – a very unaccustomed event in the Soviet Union. Not everyone is ready for such public revelations. 'We are afraid, because we can feel those who lie in wait for us, watching us with wolves' eyes, breathing down our necks – the enemies of perestroika, who gather in each other's homes in the evenings, huddled in their kitchens to condemn what is going on and prepare lists: "Our turn will come." . . . '[10] Other readers are bewildered by this display of different viewpoints; they find the discussion too muddling: 'Just tell us what we ought to think about this or that problem.'[11] For this section of the public, glasnost has an educational role to play, preparing them for a measure of tolerance. But the main reason for the popularity of magazines such as *Ogonek* or *Moscow News,* intended mainly for foreign propaganda,[12] lies in people's curiosity about the scandals revealed in them. For members of the ordinary public who witnessed such events, yesterday's secrets were no secrets at all and were passed around by word of mouth, starting rumours. Today, these periodicals are probing some of the murkier areas of Soviet life and helping remove obstacles to restructuring.

PERESTROIKA AND POLITICAL INNOVATION

The word *perestroika* refers to all the processes of renovation and restructuring of all the country's institutions. Given the Party's leading role – since it claims to be the central source of all initiative – it is its own reform that is proving most problematic. As Gorbachev has said, 'The Party must not lag behind the process now taking place in society. . . . It is the authentic organizer and true vanguard of that society. I do not think there is anyone who believes that we can do without it.'[13] One might have expected the

new Party statutes approved at the twenty-seventh congress in 1986 would introduce major changes and be dis-
cussed in the spirit of glasnost. In fact, they modified only
minor points. The statutes no longer speak of 'developed
socialism' to refer to the present stage, as under Brezhnev.
The alterations separate the work of the Party from that of
the state, and they raise the age of entry to the Party for
Komsomol applicants from twenty-three to twenty-five.
They make no change in the procedures for appointing
leaders, who at all levels continue to be co-opted, and no
limit is set to the number of times an official's term of office
may be renewed.[14]

At the Central Committee plenum of June 1987, Gorbachev proposed to institute multiple candidacies for elections to the leading organs of the Party, but this proposal
was dropped from the final resolutions. Only the new statutes of the Komsomols contain a reference to multiple
candidacies for official positions.

Nothing was definitely settled, pending a special party
conference scheduled for June 1988 to discuss reorganization of the Party. Before this, there was to be an extensive
renewal of cadres, pursuing the 'cleanup' begun by Andropov. Even before the twenty-seventh congress, 70 per
cent of ministers and 50 per cent of first secretaries in the
republics had been removed. The congress then went on to
renew 41 per cent of its members, compared with 13 per
cent in 1981 and 11 per cent in 1976, pending the day
when the Central Committee is invested with broader powers of initiative and discussion, as called for by Gorbachev.

The Party cleanup has restored some of its credibility,
by ridding it of incompetent or corrupt members. The
broom has swept very widely in certain republics, where
the leaders had established veritable fiefs, filling key posts
with members of their own families.[15] Nor has the administration been spared. It is reckoned that more than 200,000
people were prosecuted for corruption in 1986. Trade Ministry officials have been implicated in the illegal sale of

imported goods.[16] The entire staff of the Ministry for Cotton Production in Uzbekistan has been sacked for falsifying statements of acreage under plantation and cotton harvests. Manipulating statistics is commonplace in a system where arbitrary performance targets are set. On the macroeconomic level, this produces grossly inflated production figures. Two Soviet statisticians have revealed the artificiality of official statistics: the national income of the USSR in fact grew by only 6 or 7 times, between 1928 and 1985, instead of the officially announced multiples of 4.4 between 1929 and 1940, and 16.8 between 1940 and 1945.[17] The Central Statistical Office of the USSR (CSU) was reorganized in 1987 to form a new State Committee on Statistics answerable to the Council of Ministers of the USSR and the republics (Gorkomstat SSSR).

How can these practices be stopped? 'Who will rid our factory managers, and particularly the biggest among them, of their feudal mentality, their caste-ridden arrogance, and this assurance that they are there to stay, that they rule by divine right, that they are above the law and criticism? . . . Those who have the strength and the right, by which I mean the people who make up the rank and file. How? Through openness, democracy, and true, unfettered elections from the base to the top of the hierarchy.'[18] We have seen that the Party looks askance at these proposals. It has misgivings too over the idea of electing factory supervisors above the rank of foreman or brigade leader. 'Many bosses do not want to lose the right to hire or fire their subordinates, as if it had been proposed to chop off their arms. They are afraid the workers' collectives may elect someone who will not be under their thumb or who will dare to criticize them. Some managers are kept in place only by friends in high places; elections would spell disaster for them. They prefer to hide behind the principle that elections and unified management would be incompatible.'[19]

This entire system of multiple-candidate elections is

still in an experimental stage; not only have procedures
for the nomination of candidates not been settled, but
even where they have been introduced voters have not
yet mastered this new possibility: they have grown so accustomed to voting for the person they are told to vote
for, and they are unfamiliar with managers or officials
from outside their own district. The first all-Union test
came with the latest elections to the local soviets in June
1987, when voters were free to choose between several
candidates in 5 per cent of constituencies. In those cases,
voters were given a list of candidates and invited to cross
out the names they did not want; the winner was the
candidate with more than 50 per cent of votes.[20] It is
said that one of the unlucky candidates in Moscow was
the manager of the university canteen: student voters
were signaling their dissatisfaction with the food.[21] The
directors of research institutes too are now subject to
election, but this does not necessarily imply that change
is everywhere the order of the day, since in today's climate of uncertainty, many people prefer a clever conservative to an inexperienced innovator.

In the debate on the principle of holding elections to
positions of responsibility, some people have suggested
that the difficulties of appointing cadres could be overcome
by organizing competitions similar to the ones held to
recruit scientific researchers or appoint experts. The implied regulation of the status of cadres would be absolutely
in keeping with the trend to professionalization in the civil
service, run by a general Civil Service Department under
the authority of the Council of Ministers, with formal rules
of promotion and a hierarchy of functions and conditions
of employment.[22]

It is too soon to form an overall opinion of this institutional restructuring process, for it is still embryonic. Some
laws, such as the one instituting a people's referendum, or
another that allows citizens to seek redress in the courts

against the decisions of Party officials, have not yet come into effect. Furthermore, while the law regarding the principal state committees – such as Gosplan (planning), Gossnab (industrial supply), and the State Committee for Science and Technology – has been overhauled, it has yet to be promulgated.

Priority has been given to the key sectors, in line with calls to simplify the central machinery and co-ordinate complementary activities more effectively. Organs recently established include a new state committee for the information sciences; a super-ministry for the mechanical engineering industries, which combines eleven former sectoral ministries; a super-ministry of energy combining four branch ministries; and the Gosagroprom, which since 1986 has placed all the former ministries concerned with agriculture, the food processing industries and food marketing, and agricultural machinery under a unified authority in order to speed up implementation of the food program. Lastly, since 1987 a general inspectorate of product quality (Gospriemka) has been set up, with responsibility for overseeing the products of the mechanical engineering industry. The construction industry too has been reorganized, but in this case it has been decentralized, with the setting up of four new federal ministries of construction, each covering a particular region, under the supervision of a State Committee of the USSR for Construction (Gosstroi).[23] The two most recent super-ministries are the Council of Ministers of the USSR Bureau for Social Development, which oversees the administrations responsible for health, education, and labour, and a new Ministry of External Relations, which combines the functions of the former Ministry of Foreign Affairs with those of the state committee of the same name. Other administrative cuts are being contemplated.[24] So the central economic machinery has been streamlined, and it now remains to be seen what policies it is about to pursue.

ECONOMIC REFORM AND
FASTER GROWTH

Official documents describe the economic reform as radical (*korennaya perestroika*), although so far they are still discussing only preliminaries.[25] Gorbachev reckons it will take fifteen years to complete the program. But the broad lines can already be identified in the statements of Gorbachev and his main idea man, Abel Aganbegyan.[26] From these it emerges that measures taken so far, or contemplated, are designed to achieve two prime objectives:

- To speed economic growth by modernizing industry, which has fallen behind in the technological race.
- To meet the needs of production and consumption in full, so as to do away with shortages, replacing command methods of administration by economic regulation and more democratic management in the workplace.

The twelfth five-year plan (1986–90), approved by the twenty-seventh congress in 1986, set a target of boosting growth from the 3 per cent rate achieved in 1981–85 to 4–5 per cent per year. To reverse the slowing growth rate,[27] investment will concentrate on a handful of leading-edge sectors, namely chemicals, computers, biotechnology, new materials, and, more specifically, mechanical engineering, owing to the extent of the plant and machinery needing to be modernized.[28] Too much capacity lies idle due to lack of personnel, while millions of workers perform manual tasks or are kept busy repairing shoddy goods. The state intends to continue to direct investment, research, and development; the task of setting the obligations and priorities of enterprises will remain in the hands of the central organs.

The state gives the orders, but it is the enterprise that

creates wealth. The enterprise has become so entangled in a web of directives that it has lost all sense of initiative, content to take life as it comes, safe in the knowledge that the state will pick up the bill and pay the wages of its workers. The reform of the enterprise that came into force in January 1988 represents a further attempt to alter the climate of labour relations, by substituting customer demand for administrative diktat, and by tying take-home pay to the financial performance of the enterprise. The state remains the principal client: it sets priorities, sets prices, and sets the amounts to be paid into the state budget in taxes on profits and charges for the use of natural resources.[29] These amounts will be fixed for a five-year period, so as to allow the enterprise to retain any additional profit that it may earn.[30] The revenues of the enterprise are supposed to cover its operating expenses, notably wages and salaries. This internal funding will obviate the need for subsidies and result in the closing of unprofitable concerns. The enterprise will obtain its liquidity funds from the banks.

The enterprise will plan its production schedules on the basis of orders received from the state and other customers, but it will be free to decide on its techniques and suppliers. This will entail maintaining horizontal commercial relations, in place of the existing administrative system, which relies on supply through the Gossnab channels. Certain firms will be authorized even to have direct dealings with foreign organizations.[31] The biggest enterprises will be attached directly to the central overseeing body, but the others will be organized into 'complexes', in combinations appropriate to their particular line of business. So the enterprise will remain under supervision, but its earnings will henceforward depend solely on the reputation of its output.

In order to trigger the change in attitude needed to mobilize the 'human factor', wages are to be tied to the

financial performance of the enterprise. The State Committee for Labour and Wages will set stable norms, which will
in turn set the size of the wage fund and lay down recommendations regarding its use; bonuses, on the other hand,
will be the exclusive preserve of the enterprise itself. The
current tendency is to give greater importance to wages as
a percentage of total earnings, and to broaden the range of
pay to the benefit of the engineer – whose salary has gone
up by 30 to 40 per cent[32] – to generalize the payment of
collective bonuses to the brigade or workshop as a whole,
which is then apportioned according to each worker's contribution. The increased role of the workers' collective,
especially in the planned election of managers, forms part
of the series of measures designed to involve workers in the
management of their enterprise, since their performance
will henceforward condition not merely their pay, but also
the resources available for social benefits (housing, cultural
and sports amenities, vacation camps, etc.).

Because living conditions are largely the responsibility
of the soviets, these authorities are being provided with
proper management at the provincial (oblast) level, so as
to co-ordinate social programs and make sure that they are
properly funded – through income taxes levied on the
enterprises in their area, and through fines raised from
polluting factories. Efforts are being made also to channel
the savings of factory and kolkhoz workers into social
schemes, via bonds or other loans 'for which levying norms
have yet to be laid down',[33] which points to the introduction of a compulsory levy on inflationary earnings.[34]

The most awkward of all problems is that of prices,
because so long as prices do not reflect true costs, the
profitability of an enterprise, and hence its workers' remu-
neration, will not necessarily reflect improved management. The trouble is that if, as Gorbachev has announced,
prices are to be made to reflect costs, then it is going to be
necessary to abolish 73 billion rubles in subsidies and to

raise retail prices by some 60 billion rubles (the amount currently being spent to keep food prices at their present level).

Price reform is proving difficult not only because of its impact on the cost of living, but also because economists disagree as to whether priority should be given to greater social justice or to rectifying existing price distortions in order to stimulate the economy. Whatever they decide, price reform presupposes a measure of control over inflation, failing which, the expected rise in prices could trigger an uncontrollable spiral.

The 'deficit' — which is the material expression of this inflation — flows from the surplus of liquidity over the supply of goods and services, due to the fact that enterprises can too easily resort to credit to cover their short-term cash and capital expenditure needs. That is how the banks put the savings deposited with them to work; they feed on inflation. A reform of the banking system is under way to set ceilings on banks' commitments and create a capital market to attract private savings. The Savings and Loan Bank, which has replaced the older savings banks, now offers investments in the form of 250-, 500-, and 1,000-ruble certificates yielding 4 per cent interest; but there is also talk of offering the public stock in enterprises and co-operatives.

Government administrations have not waited until 1991 to proceed, in keeping with facilities offered by the 1987 enterprise law with respect to 'contractual' prices, to jack up their tariffs as they see fit (for telephones, stamps, public transport, bathhouses, movie theatres, toothpaste, and even bread). Attempts to regulate the economy by prices would run into difficulties in the absence of a free market, given the monopoly that enterprises and government administrations generally enjoy for certain goods and services.

Measures to improve the situation in agriculture are

based primarily on giving workers a financial stake in raising output.[35] Experience has convinced Gorbachev that contracts based on the output of autonomous teams – and that can include members of a single family (*kollektivnyi podryad na semeinoi osnove*) – are a highly effective means of boosting productivity and bringing down production costs.[36] The ambitious investment schemes of the 1970s proved to be cash drains; however, there is no intention of abandoning efforts to develop the non-black-earth lands.[37] Since 1986, moreover, the kolkhoz and sovkhoz are entitled to market up to 30 per cent of their planned production in the town markets – and all of their surpluses.

A new status was approved for the kolkhoz in March 1988, which introduces a number of innovations regarding the size of family farms.[38] Their area and the number of livestock are no longer subject to uniform norms for each republic, but will henceforth be set by the assembly of each kolkhoz 'depending on the contribution of its members to collective work'. This old-style wording reflects fears that family activities may unduly distract the peasants. Curiously, nothing is said about subcontracting between the family farms and the kolkhoz (*semeinyi podryad* – 'family contract', not to be confused with 'family team'). Since the current tendency is to refer to the co-operative tradition dear to Lenin, one might have thought that these new legislative measures would have left greater freedom to the kolkhoz; in fact, what counts in the eyes of the authorities is less the assembly than the way the chairmen are appointed. Judging by reactions reported in the press, the administration has not relaxed its tutelage over the kolkhoz. It still lays down the quantities to be handed over and sets prices; the kolkhozes are free only in regard to the remainder of their output, which means that their production plan cannot be framed on the basis of profitability, but solely on the basis of the state's requirements, which continue to take priority.

The freedoms offered to the family sector – which will permit savings in public investment in order to achieve rapid results – are applicable only in regions such as the Caucasus and Central Asia, where families are still large enough (averaging five people) to be capable of farming 50–100 hectares. It is hard to see how this formula could appeal to the peasantry in the deserted villages of the RSFSR (Russia), where the peasant has lost the ancestral custom of working from dawn to dusk and is wary of a possible reversal of the present policy favoring the private sector, as has happened in the past.

The second leg of Soviet policy to improve consumption takes the form of the decisions – unprecedented since the New Economic Policy (NEP) of the 1920s – to encourage individual and co-operative activities, inspired by the example of certain of the people's democracies. Before legalizing certain individual economic activities (by the statutory instrument of 19 November 1986), which had already proliferated in the parallel economy, a statute was issued on 28 May 1986 to bolster repression of illegal traders – that is, any jobless person earning an income. This initially created some confusion at the local level, and it bred some excesses on the part of the authorities against peasants, for fear that they would desert collective labour for the private sector. Since 1 May 1987, family agriculture has ceased to be the only sector open to individual economic activity: some thirty or so small-scale industrial or service activities are now permitted, provided they are declared to the authorities.[39] They are subject to fairly heavy taxes (up to 65 per cent of the upper income band, against a 13 per cent maximum tax on salaried earnings). But that does not appear to deter applicants.[40] According to some estimates, 5 to 8 million people could be legally engaged in these co-operative or private sectors. By 1 December 1987, some 828 co-operatives had been approved, and 8,000 citizens had been granted artisan's licenses. The total number of people employed in the nonagricultural co-operative sector had risen tenfold to 150,000 at the end of 1987, but this development has not yet had any impact on the price of individual services, which remain very high.

Abel Aganbegyan has warned against the illusions (*samo-obman*) of those who expect restructuring of the economy to yield rapid results. The USSR is not going to renew two-thirds of its stock of machine tools overnight, he says, or build the 40 million new homes it needs if it is to provide each Soviet family with a home of its own, or retrain cadres and managers still ill-prepared for the new responsibilities being laid upon them.[41] The reform now in progress is a long-term affair, and its success will depend not only on the resources available, but also on the capacity for change of the social groups involved in the production process.

Military spending cuts are a prerequisite of an investment recovery. Discarding the present system of supplying industry and the transition to a market in industrial goods – something the Soviet Union has never managed to introduce even though it has been on the agenda since 1963 – presupposes an end to shortages. Officials hope that the abolition of rationing will unfreeze some 460 billion rubles' worth (Aganbegyan's estimate) of inventories being hoarded by enterprises in anticipation of shortages – which in turn merely create shortages of their own. On the consumer-goods side, shortages have led to rationing in many towns and to rocketing unregulated prices. The knottiest problem is going to be the return to real prices for foodstuffs as subsidies are removed. Tatyana Zaslavskaya would also like, in the name of social justice, to see an end to disparities in purchasing power between the large cities – where prices are subsidized – and the other towns, where co-operatives charge much higher prices.[42] It will presumably be necessary to offset price rises by increasing the lowest wages. All these difficulties explain why reform of the price and credit system, and of the system of supplying enterprises, has been put off until 1990.

The social ramifications and political obstacles to be overcome are no less great, for unprofitable enterprises are going to have to either close or lay off workers. L. Aboltin estimates that some 15 million jobs will have to go in industry, construction, and transportation. The sharpest resistance is coming from the administration. Ministries and cadres have no wish to be stripped of their power, nor are they prepared to shoulder heavy responsibilities; they prefer to shelter behind dogma. They are backed in this by the military, who are anxious to preserve the privileged status of the arms industry. This may account for the protracted timetable for reform and the ambiguity of the official documents on the reform of the enterprise, which can be interpreted 'so that one section rectifies the previous one'.[43] We may regard this as a sign of a desire for compromise, or rather a desire to maintain the Party's leading role in the economy. In fact, though, the past and present directions of the twelfth five-year plan are imposed by the central authorities, not by some socialist market. So far, there has been no fundamental change in the workings of the planned economy. 'We have not made any proposal that steps beyond the bounds of the planned economy,' said Gorbachev. 'Our intention is not to replace socialism by some other system, but to reinforce it.'[44]

So we cannot form any definitive judgement of the real changes that have occurred until 1990, when the new powers of Gosplan and Gossnab are to be announced, together with procedures for the reform of prices and credit.

For the time being, according to factory managers, there is no autonomy.[45] Gorbachev has said that 'the Party cannot relinquish its leading role in the economy,' notably as regards the choice of priorities and the appointments to positions of responsibility;[46] and he is losing patience with resistance in the bureaucracy: 'Change is proceeding too slowly; it is time to call the foot-draggers to account.'[47] But he knows too that the outcome of the battle depends not only on the general staff, but on the rank and file as well. 'Society is made up of concrete forces: the working class, the peasants, the intellectuals, each of which has its respective interests. One cannot infuse dynamism into society or make it viable if one ignores the interests of these social groups, and if these interests do not influence our policy in return.'[48] We now need to analyse this feedback from society in response to the reforms that Gorbachev has envisaged.

3

■

SOVIET SOCIETY
AND CHANGE

■

■ Decrees have never in themselves been capable of changing society radically. Society changes when the behaviour of individuals is affected by a deep-seated change in social values. The new values can prevail only when they have the backing of social forces – whether they are classes or coalitions of interests – sufficiently powerful to ensure the triumph of their demands or aspirations. Although in the Soviet Union the reforms are being imposed from the top down, rather than the reverse, it is worth looking at how far the different sections of society are capable of changing and at how they are reacting to these reforms. This task is complicated by the fact that the different components of Soviet society are unable to express themselves openly, other than within the limits tolerated by glasnost. Here, therefore, we shall have to confine ourselves to what is visible on the surface, in the form of open discussions, without claiming to assess the true extent of the underlying currents.

In place of the official division of Soviet society into three classes – workers, peasants, and intellectuals – we have preferred to divide them into three categories corresponding to the respective degrees to which each group is able to influence change: (1) the people – the peasants and workers; (2) the elite – the decision-makers and creative workers; (3) the marginal elements, such as youthful rebels and dissidents.

THE PEOPLE

THE PEASANTRY

Until not so long ago, the peasantry was the largest group in the country; today, it is a residual population made up of those who have not managed to get away from the countryside. The peasantry is no longer one of the main driving forces of society, nor is it any longer homogeneous. Alongside the great mass of peasants (mostly women who have no specialized skills) who perform manual tasks in the fields or the cowsheds, there is a stratum of much-better-paid tractor mechanics (mostly men) and specialists (agronomists, schoolteachers, medical auxiliaries) who form a sort of rural intelligentsia, but whose education and lifestyle bring them much closer to the people living in the towns, which is where they were trained. Lastly, at the pinnacle of the village hierarchy stand the officials – the kolkhoz chairman, the managers of the sovkhoz, the Party cadres – who serve as intermediaries between town and country.

In the eyes of the latter, orders handed down from the *raikom* (the Party's district organization) and the RAPO (district agro-industrial union) are always out of touch with the specific conditions of each region. These local worthies have seen too many such 'experiments' and 'campaigns' imposed on them from above not to cast a slightly jaundiced eye at the new line. So operations managers go on grumbling at having to obey yet another set of unfair or ill-judged directives, and they have to pay additional taxation in kind to offset the shortfalls of laggardly farmers. They would have preferred a stable tax in kind. Far from improving matters, the formation of the Agroprom has served merely to strengthen the grip of the bureaucracy. The operations managers' lack of autonomy reflects the authorities' age-old mistrust of the peasantry.

Past traumas suffered at the time of collectivization and after the war, when the kolkhozes were combined (in the 1950s) and above all when villages were regrouped (in the 1960s), are frequently mentioned by local writers in explaining the apathy and frustrations of this downtrodden population that has given its finest sons to the motherland. Many never returned from the war, and others preferred to look for better-paid work in the towns or on the great construction projects. For a tractor driver, working on a nationally famous project brought status; staying behind on the kolkhoz brought neither respect nor a future.

What could the authorities do to re-instill in the peasant a feeling that he was master in his own house, of being the 'boss' (*khozyain*)? As we have seen, Gorbachev's policies are designed to motivate workers by organizing them into autonomous teams – made up of members of a single family if need be – and broadening the scope for individual economic activity. However, the way in which these directives are applied is to some extent left to the discretion of local officials. Consequently, the reactions of the peasants differ from one region to another, depending on the degree of latitude left to the family sector. For example, the recent law allowing kolkhozians to own a horse is applicable throughout the RSFSR, but it is rarely applied in Byelorussia. In Georgia and Azerbaijan, on the other hand, three-quarters of the horses are privately owned; in Central Asia, mares may be owned solely for the purpose of making koumiss.

In regions such as Kazakhstan, where despite the rehabilitation of the Akshi method – assigning work to small autonomous teams, and rewarding them according to their production – the authorities have shown little haste in implementing it, resistance has been encountered, leading Gorbachev to insist in June 1987 on the benefits of organizing the work in autonomous teams. Elsewhere, it is feared that the freedoms granted to the private sector could trigger a flood of farm labour to more lucrative occupations and away from collective work (certain hothouse cucumber growers in Ukraine earn up to 13,000 rubles a month, while others are hiring labour under cover of fictitious co-operatives).[1] The authorities are afraid too of accusations of corruption, of fostering the emergence of a kulak class; consequently they are applying the decree of May 1986, which punishes speculation, with greater zeal than the decree of November 1986, which legalizes many individual occupations.

Whereas in the Baltic lands measures to ease restrictions on the peasantry have been most clearly understood and applied most intelligently, in the southern regions a brutal campaign has been launched against families – often pensioners – who grow fruit and vegetables in greenhouses for sale at market: the local authorities have called in the militia to help ruin them, cutting off the water supply of those who refuse to obey. In certain districts in the province of Volgograd, the militia charged women who had come to sell their tomatoes on the river landing stages, and they threw up roadblocks to prohibit access to the markets. 'Are Tomatoes Criminal?' asked a headline in *Literaturnaya Gazeta*, over an article relating these incidents[2] – which seems to show that such measures are not approved by the central government. But they do reveal the climate that still prevails in the countryside: the peasant is still the 'villain' of the piece, suspected of base motives and still subject to the whims of local potentates whom no authority appears to be capable of controlling. 'These people have turned their districts or kolkhozes into veritable private domains,' Gorbachev has said.[3]

Nor do the advantages extended to the peasants do much to improve their relations with the townspeople. The latter are jealous of those peasants who have grown rich by trade and now drive around in a car, and who charge exorbitant prices in the markets.[4] They grumble at being forced to go and help with the harvest or at being mobilized to sort vegetables while the kolkhozians throng the markets, forgetting that life for the kolkhozian has not always been a bed of roses and that they too have a right to live in comfort in return for their backbreaking work.

THE WORKERS

In his inaugural speech to the eighteenth congress of the Trade Unions of the USSR in February 1987, Gorbachev noted that his policies had been encountering resistance, and he expressed his confidence in the support of the workers to offset, through self-management, the influence of the technocrats in the bureaucracy. In his view, the labour unions had the potential to become 'a force for framing legislative proposals in the social sphere', although nothing has been done yet to modify the powers of the unions. It is not that the blue-collar workers have no opinion on what is happening, but passiveness and skepticism are the dominant attitudes. Some months later, Gorbachev learned, in his meetings with workers, that they were puzzled: 'When is perestroika going to reach us, Mikhail Sergeivich?'[5] They are not hostile to the reforms, but they do think they are too slow in materializing.

The hardest thing for perestroika to overcome is apathy, 'because we've heard this kind of thing before, and we have persuaded ourselves that the bureaucracy is an insurmountable obstacle.'[6] Public opinion is reacting cautiously, and many people fear that their criticisms could rebound on them. In spite of the law passed in 1985 that protects them in principle from possible reprisals, they say that the courts 'judge the relative importance of the litigants according to their position'. Which is why, although fewer letters of complaint are anonymous than used to be the case, signatories still ask for their names to be omitted for fear that the present policy could be reversed.

The traditionally apolitical outlook of the blue-collar workers is evident in what they read and in their lack of interest in lectures on Party life or on 'scientific communism'. At Taganrog, a city of 290,000 inhabitants, the regional press has more readers than the big national papers, and a sports periodical, *Sovetskii Sport,* has by far the most subscribers. In this city, more than half the people interviewed were unable to understand the commonest terms in the political vocabulary, such as 'opposition', 'monopoly', 'militarization', 'reactionary', 'liberal', 'forces of the left'; only 54 per cent were able to define more or less correctly the word 'imperialism'.[7] Generally speaking, people's interest in public life increases with the level of their educational qualifications. Specialists play a more active part than blue-collar workers in civic activities. An opinion poll taken by a French polling firm in Moscow, applying Western methods to a sample of 1,000 people, showed that over 80 per cent of respondents favoured multiple candidacies at local elections, restrictions on the sale of alcohol, and the election of factory managers by the workers themselves.[8]

When questioned, not about principles, but about the implementation of measures, workers are more critical: they say that their managers do not keep them informed, and that the administration selects those candidates for elections that best suit its needs (*vygodnye*); voting procedures afford voters no anonymity, and people are afraid to go into the booth to cross out a candidate's name. Only 38 per cent of the workers interviewed acknowledged that glasnost has changed the climate of labour relations; the majority remark that, as in the past, they continue to work on the basis of 'you scratch my back, I'll scratch yours'.[9]

In spite of everything, workers with grievances did not

wait until glasnost to express them in letters to the newspapers. Before 1985, letters complaining about living conditions (food, housing, public health) outnumbered complaints about working conditions (pay, safety at work, relations with superiors). On none of these items can perestroika bring about any rapid improvement. Indeed, working conditions are going to become more stringent, while the housing crisis, which is affecting all the big cities apart from the capital, cannot be overcome before the end of the century.[10] In Khrushchev's time, the Soviet Union achieved a construction rate of 121 units per 10,000 inhabitants in 1960; by 1985 this figure had fallen to 72 per 10,000. This means that the number of apartments built annually (2 million) is less than the number of couples marrying or divorcing in a year (respectively 2.8 million and 950,000). Qualitative improvements alone are expected in the thirty or so big cities, where Gospriemka, the State Commission for Standards, has been given the task of supervising approval of newly built buildings, provided it adopts the point of view of the future tenants rather than that of the buildings' trustees.

Housing is allocated parsimoniously, and not always fairly. Many complaints against abuses and favouritism end up in the courts. The government has felt impelled to make clear that the leaders' own domestic servants (chauffeurs, secretaries, etc.) are no longer supposed to enjoy priority treatment. Those who do not have the means to buy a co-operative apartment have put their names down on long waiting lists: ten years in Magnitogorsk and Sverdlovsk, fifteen in Kaluga; in the Moscow suburb of Stupino, people moving into apartments in 1987 had gone on the waiting lists in the 1960s. In Leningrad, most of the population still live in communal apartments;[11] those living as tenants of private landlords pay monthly rentals of 30 to 50 rubles (the lowest-paid workers earn less than 100 rubles per month). Three-quarters of young couples go to live with their parents after their marriage. The worst-housed are the workers living in hostels (*obshchezhitie*) built for bachelors, where the cramped conditions and promiscuity are barely tolerable.[12]

There has been no improvement in supplies of food or other goods. Queues and food rationing are the daily lot of most citydwellers. In 1987, the people of Magnitogorsk were entitled to one kilogram of meat and 400 grams of butter per person per month.[13] Many blue-collar and white-collar workers have a small plot of ground on the outskirts of the city, where they grow vegetables. The demand for land is so great that it will take two to three years to meet. Measures taken since 1985 to step up the fight against alcoholism — by limiting liquor production and restricting the hours during which it can be sold[14] — have led to the disappearance of eau de cologne from the perfume stores, while sugar too has become scarce, as it is used to make moonshine liquor (*samogon*). There are reports of endless queues outside the liquor stores,[15] due to the government's unwillingness to ration vodka in the big cities. At Petrozavodsk (Karelia), where rationing was tried, the measure had to be rescinded because taxis were going as far as Murmansk and Leningrad in search of vodka, and because the old peasant women in the country-side, for lack of either vodka or coupons for it, were no longer able to give tractor drivers who came to plow their garden the customary bottle.[16]

Although some opinion polls suggest that the population favors these measures, they are too much at odds with social habits and family traditions to be popular.[17] A 1985 survey of eleven regions of the USSR showed that only 21 per cent of respondents viewed alcoholism as a disease; the majority approved the measures to limit its consumption in public places, but they took a more lenient view than the authorities of its distillation and consumption in the home. In 1986, officials confiscated 900,000 illicit stills and convicted more than 200,000 black-market dealers or distill-ers. The same survey showed that, contrary to a wide-spread misapprehension, drink is not a part of youth culture: 51 per cent of young people do not drink until they reach age twenty, when they start their first job and come into contact with older workers. People drink more often with their colleagues than with their families, except in republics such as Georgia or Moldavia, where making and drinking wine are part of an ancient national tradition.[18] The most widespread public view is that administrative measures will be incapable of successfully tackling a prob-lem whose roots are as deep as they are varied.

No less worrying than the restrictions on vodka sales are the increases in the prices of foodstuffs announced by Gorbachev at Murmansk in October 1987, which pose a threat to the workers' purchasing power. The elimination of budget subsidies (equivalent to 60 billion rubles) is supposed to be accompanied by a rise in the lowest salaries and in government benefits – but will that be enough to make up for the price rises, which could lead to a doubling of today's prices for certain items such as meat?[19]

Further, the reform of wages, which provides for the introduction of quality controls in certain industries, is by no means popular. Because these controls are not applied across the board, those subject to them feel unfairly penal-ized, especially as some of the defects are blamed on the supplier. Bonuses are no longer paid automatically but are tied to productivity gains; in an autonomous brigade, this means that the brigade leader's say in how the bonuses are shared out places the worker in a position of dependence, which could give rise to abuses.[20] In a word, the days when the worker could work in a climate of generalized laxness are over.

The abolition of subsidies to industry will also lead to the closing of several thousand enterprises,[21] or at best to layoffs as firms seek ways to balance their books and generate funds internally. Almost a third of the nation's enterprises are said to be in this position.[22] So far, there have been reports of only isolated cases of factory closings; but the firing of 12,000 railroad workers in Byelorussia when internal funding was introduced did spark protests.[23] In 1986, the ten railroad lines fired 125,000 workers. Over the next fifteen years, some 15 to 16 million industrial and agricultural workers are expected to have to change jobs.[24] Under present regulations, workers laid off for economic reasons are entitled to three months' severance.[25] Other dangers loom on the horizon if, as has been mooted, certain of the higher-paid categories lose their entitlements to free social services.[26] Medical care for a fee has already made its appearance in Moscow.[27]

Talk of undoing the achievements ascribed to socialism, such as job security and welfare, and calls for higher productivity from workers without any immediate compensation, are scarcely calculated to stir the enthusiasm of the workers. Most of them say they are only vaguely familiar with the reforms, and they are reluctant to speak their minds, because they know from experience that 'loud-mouths' are likely to get short shrift from their superiors.[28] 'Democratization' has not yet modified the climate of labour relations. Sporadic strikes have greeted attempts to tinker with the bonus system; they may have been short-lived, but they are growing more frequent, and for the first time they are rating a mention in the Soviet press.[29]

WOMEN: A NEW CONSCIOUSNESS
It is among women than one finds the greatest approval of the authorities' efforts to combat speculation, corruption, and alcoholism. In recent decades, Soviet women have displayed the clearest outward signs of change, not only in their concern with elegance, which is making them more demanding and whetting their curiosity about fashion,[30] but also in their pressing of specific demands. Zoya Bogus-

lavskaya remarks bitterly that one still sees few women in the Soviet foreign service or at international congresses, and far too many wielding shovels along the roads or wheelbarrows on construction sites, while men control the machinery.[31] Women are less and less inclined to put up with this inequality, because it goes hand in hand with additional chores for mothers in the home. New attitudes are becoming commonplace, as women accept the idea of having a baby but not the shackles of marriage; they want a shorter working day for women in order to compensate for the time they spend on family obligations.[32]

It is presumably in response to women's specific problems and to incite them to play an active part in perestroika that one of the institutions from the earliest days of the revolution is about to be revived, namely the local women's councils (*zhensovety*). Will these assemblies be powerful enough to counteract the excessively male vision of the rights of men and women that has hitherto predominated in the USSR?

THE ELITES

THE OFFICER CORPS

The army is the symbol of the nation and the sufferings it endured during the last war. Also it is the material expression of the most advanced achievements of Soviet science and technology. It has always been the government's top priority in the allocation of resources, and its officers are more highly paid than ministers.

The political and military training that officers receive in the special schools, with their long-established traditions, help to forge an esprit de corps. Of all the institutions of the USSR, it is in the higher reaches of the armed forces that this esprit de corps is strongest. This does not facilitate dialogue with young recruits, with their libertarian ideas.

Consequently, officers can be expected to take a dim view of glasnost and its incitements to overstep taboos. Last but not least, Gorbachev's nuclear-disarmament initiatives, with their implied threat of possible military spending cuts, are a further cause for discontent.

This might explain why Gorbachev has issued a reminder to the army of the need for discipline and vigilance,[33] and why, after the young German Mathias Rust had landed his light aircraft in the middle of Red Square, on 28 May 1987, Boris Yeltsin, until recently Moscow Party secretary, went still further and denounced 'the refusal of the military to become involved in the reforms, their allergy to anything new, their contempt for human dignity, their arrogance and self-satisfaction, their favouritism, personal whims, elitism'.[34]

Could this be the sign of a conflict between the civilian and the military authorities? To think so would be to argue as if the army were outside the Party. In fact, the officer corps is an integral part of the Party, and the latter's control over the high command has been made plain — notably in September 1984, with the demotion of General Ogarkov, who had been chief of staff when the Korean airliner was shot down a year earlier. More recently, the Rust affair led to the retirement of Defense Minister General Sokolov, and to sanctions against high-ranking generals such as the head of air defenses, A. Koldunov. A few weeks earlier, on 4 May 1987, the minster of civil aviation, Marshal Boris Bugayev, had been sacked because of the high incidence of Aeroflot accidents.

The fact remains, however, that if the officer corps is a component of the Party, it has inevitably become embroiled in its quarrels; consequently, the high command is not immune from the splits that occur within the Party at times of crisis. In such cases, the army may hold the tie-breaking vote when conflicts arise, as happened at the beginning and end of Khrushchev's reign. According to certain rumours, Romanov enjoyed support in the military-industrial establishment, but this was not enough to carry the day against Gorbachev. The prestige of the army took some knocks when it was bogged down in Afghanistan, and following the dubious showing of Soviet equipment in the Middle East. An elite corps never likes to feel that its image has been dented. So Gorbachev deemed it politic to reassert 'solemnly, in the Politburo and the Defense Council' – of which he is chairman – 'that there cannot be the slightest doubt as to the capacity of the armed forces of the USSR to defend the country', to avoid any hard feelings that may have arisen following the Rust affair.

On the borderline between the civilian and the military sectors – a borderline does not exist at the top, since civilians such as Brezhnev and Ustinov had been promoted to the highest rank in the military machine – stand the top people in the military-industrial complex. They take an indulgent view of economic reforms, provided they do not threaten the priority currently enjoyed by the arms industry and are designed to improve the efficiency of the economy as a whole, because contrary to a widespread misconception, the military sector does not operate in a vacuum and is in fact heavily dependent on the civilian industries. Their attitude would be very different if foreign-policy initiatives were to lead to military-spending cuts: opponents would find powerful support in the military establishment.

THE *NOMENKLATURA:* MISGIVINGS

The Party's general secretary makes no secret of the fact that, notwithstanding surface approval, his reforms are encountering formidable inertia, and even resistance, in the bureaucracy: 'A sometimes secret, but inflexible, struggle of ideas and habits is going on. Those who cling to the past won't give up without a fight.'[35] His tone grows increasingly harsh when he speaks of 'those who have not given up hope of burying us, of preventing us from putting an end, once and for all, to negligence, lack of foresight, injustice, corruption, and the absolute immunity of the higher echelons',[36] and of those 'who adopt an attitude of wait-and-see, or who openly throw a monkey-wrench in the works, hampering the development of political activity'.[37] He even goes so far as to speak of 'sabotage',[38] and at the Smolny Institute in Leningrad, he threatened that 'those who stand in the way of restructuring will be swept aside'.[39]

The motives of those who oppose his policies are clear: any in-depth restructuring disturbs habits and threatens privileges. The number of people who make up the *nomenklatura* is quite considerable — between 500,000 and 1.5 million, not counting the leadership (*rukovoditeli*). The 'waiters' and the opponents are recruited at all levels of the pyramid, starting with the Central Committee, more than half of whose members were appointed by Gorbachev's predecessors. Even inside the Politburo, alongside members of the old guard such as Vladimir Shcherbitsky and Andrei Gromyko, Yegor Ligachev and Viktor Chebrikov come out with certain utterances that are more than mere glosses on what Gorbachev has to say about glasnost and the history of the Party since the 1930s.[40]

There is more massive resistance in the regional echelons, because the authority of the central leadership diminishes in proportion as one travels from Moscow. A regional or local representative of the Party is a feudal baron upon whose good will everything depends, starting with appointments to *nomenklatura* posts within his bailiwick. He is surrounded by people devoted to him, and the local bureaucracy naturally stands by the boss. He thus builds up a network of clients who are obligated to him and who will be dragged down with him if ever some 'affair' should come into the open. This explains the extent of some of the recent purges, notably in Central Asia, where tribalism and nepotism are still deeply rooted.[41]

Ideology is not the most serious grounds for opposition: much more deeply felt are the attacks on privileges and the threat that glasnost poses to vested interests. These privileges, in the form of housing and official cars, special stores, etc., were the reward for the abnegation and servility demanded of Party functionaries. They had grown accustomed to being obeyed at the push of a button;[42] the local press was at their beck and call, because their merits were appreciated in high places not on account of any real results – which were unchecked because uncheckable – but in light of the reports they sent in, which were arranged to enhance their reputation. Now their reputation is liable to be tarnished overnight by some meddling journalist. The more skillful obkom secretaries themselves tell their journalists what to criticize,[43] which may explain why the provincial press is a little slow in following the lead of the Moscow press. Woe betide anyone who thought glasnost was an invitation to spill the beans about the luxury dachas of certain dignitaries or the special schools reserved for the elite.[44] The Supreme Soviet had to pass a special act in June 1987 to protect such people from reprisals.

Discontent is spreading to the administrations that are now in the 'firing line' from economic reform. 'The administrative machinery is opposed to measures that seek to strip it of certain of its powers. Some factory managers in particular are unhappy.'[45] Twenty-two thousand officials were affected by restructuring in various ministries in 1985, and another 60,000 are destined to lose their jobs by 1990.[46] In the enterprises, the most energetic managers had taken the lead in calling for the rights that have now been accorded them in the new act due to come into effect in 1988. But the majority of managers are going to have difficulty taking on new roles. For them, autonomy means freedom to acquire at their discretion the additional 'inputs' that they require, over and above the ceilings imposed on them by the planning organs. In other words, their mentality is that of the administrator. They are incapable of reasoning in terms of

economic efficiency.[47] Theirs are the motives of the official,
for whom success is measured not in terms of profit or
revenues, but in terms of fringe benefits and promotion,
access to goods, foreign travel, and a seat in the Supreme
Soviet.[48] An administrative economy in which all that is
demanded of one is obedience may be reassuring, but only a
tiny minority possess the managerial qualities to innovate
and take initiatives.[49]

Given all that, one may well ask whom Gorbachev is
counting on to apply his reforms. First of all, he is counting
on the rising generation that is taking over from the gerontocrats on the occasion of purges and as part of a general
rejuvenation of the ranks of cadres. In the province of
Omsk, almost half the urban district secretaries are now
under forty, compared with a third in 1978.[50] Even so, one
cannot reduce everything to a conflict of generations.
George Breslauer's work on the political thinking of regional (obkom) secretaries, as these may be gleaned from
articles or speeches at plenums or congresses, shows that
there is no obvious correlation between their ideas and
their age group.[51] Cleavages (and at the local level, conflicts) occur far more between officials who owe their posts
to Party membership and their ability to give orders than
to their qualifications, on the one hand, and specialists who
approach issues in terms of professional rather than political criteria, on the other.[52] Multi-candidate elections to
managerial and official posts are bound to strengthen the
position of the latter. But one is not going to persuade the
people currently occupying these posts of the virtues of
professionalism overnight, and in the meantime jealousy
and intrigue are likely to breed coalitions of interests to
hinder, or even thwart, what must surely be the inevitable
long-term outcome.

THE CREATIVE INTELLIGENTSIA: FERMENT
Gorbachev can also count on the support of a broad section
of the intelligentsia.[53] It is true to say that, so far, writers,

filmmakers, and artists have been the chief beneficiaries of perestroika. This can be seen in two types of change. The first is at the institutional level, as the heads of the different professional 'unions' are changed and the chief editors of the leading literary reviews are replaced; autonomous associations are being founded too, such as the National Fund for the Safeguarding of Culture, and increased credits are being allocated to these associations. The second area of change is in artistic creation itself, where a more liberal attitude has permitted publications, performances, and exhibitions that would formerly have been banned.

It was not very difficult to contrive changes in unions grouping members of a single profession, by placing at their head people in agreement with the policies laid down by the Secretariat of the Central Committee. The instructions had to come down from the top, since works tackling taboo subjects were published or presented before these unions were able to hold their congresses.[54] The congress of filmmakers set the ball rolling on 13–15 May 1986, when it elected Yelem Klimov as head of the union and criticized in detail the past management of the State Committee for the Film Industry (Goskino), nepotism in the film directors' schools, and the sidelining of innovators. The cleanup has spread to the editorial offices of film magazines and has succeeded in releasing films that had until now been kept out of the theatres, such as Tenghiz Abuladze's *Repentance* (*Pokayanie*).[55] The writers' congress followed, on 25–28 June 1986. The congress of theatre workers came in December 1986; they elected to their leadership Mikhail Shatrov, the author of *Dictatorship of Conscience,* a play that caused a sensation by depicting Lenin on stage. The appointment of Sergei Zalygin to the editorship of *Novy Mir,* after having been on the magazine's editorial board in the days of Tvardovsky, was another harbinger of a return to the liberal tradition. This was the magazine that published Solzhenitsyn's first works.[56] This time, it was the magazine *Druzhba Narodov* (nos. 4 to

6, 1987) which caused a sensation in publishing an equally innovative work that deals with the Stalinist purges, *The Children of the Arbat* by Anatoly Rybakov, after having been banned by the censorship for twenty-five years. Another sensation was Vassily Grossman's novel *Life and Destiny*, about the battle of Stalingrad and the genocide of Russian Jews, already published in the West and due to be published in the magazine *Oktyabr.*

At a private meeting with twenty or so writers at the Kremlin on 19 June 1986, before the opening of the eighth writers' congress, Gorbachev asked for their support in his fight for a moral cleanup, and against bureaucracy and the privileges that create a barrier between the leadership and the people.[57] He also warned them against any spirit of revenge. This warning does not appear to have been heeded, because we are now witnessing some sharp controversies between advocates and opponents of certain Soviet writers such as Vassily Belov, or émigré writers such as Nabokov.[58] Does the rehabilitation of writers such as Zamyatin, Gumilev, Babel, and Platonov, or the publication of Pasternak's *Doctor Zhivago,* [59] mean that we should now turn against the people responsible for censoring them? The authorities do not appear to be paying much attention to calls for justice, being unwilling to turn the revision of history into a series of trials.

Since the eighth writers' congress, 'socialist realism' no longer appears to be the mandatory model.[60] As Gorbachev put it, 'If you try to smooth out society with a hot iron, you're liable to drive out all talent.'[61]

Does this mean that the creative intelligentsia has definitively won its autonomy within Soviet society?

Censorship (Glavlit) has not been abolished, but according to Zalygin its role will be reduced to the control of information pertaining to security and it will cease to intervene in editorial decisions.[62] A great step would be taken toward independence if writers were to obtain the material wherewithal to run co-operative publishing ventures.

These are permitted in principle, and at least two such co-operatives have been set up recently, but they are experiencing difficulty in obtaining paper from the state; another problem is that all Soviet printing presses are controlled by the state.[63] After some hesitation, a statutory instrument of 23 October 1987 called a halt to the creation of independent publishing co-operatives. As Gorbachev said in a meeting with media representatives on 8 January 1988, 'A magazine, a publishing house, or a newspaper is not a personal affair; it is the affair of the Party.'

Without belittling the progress achieved, the fact is that, like other forms of expression, literature is still under surveillance, and the borderline between what is forbidden and what is permitted is a shifting one. All down the ages, writers and artists who have crossed that line have been excluded and condemned to a marginal existence.

THE MARGINAL ELEMENTS

YOUTH: REBELLION

Glasnost, slayer of myths, and the charismatic Gorbachev, incarnation of change and movement, ought to have struck a chord with Soviet youth. The leader is counting on young people to overcome resistance to his line.[64] Unfortunately for him, youth is a transitional stage: it is neither homogeneous nor a social force. Young people are always the ones to pass the harshest or most jaded judgements on their elders. They have a particularly fine sense of the distance between official exhortations and the realities of everyday life.[65] The Party is not immune to this hypocrisy. In a word, young people are fully behind the policy of 'cleanup', but they are naturally critical and independent-minded, and are unwilling to be enrolled under anyone's banner. Glasnost gives them greater assurance, because impertinence has become irrepressible, and they know it.

Although generalizations about youth are risky, so varied are their informal affinity groups, one does nevertheless note a number of shared characteristics:

- Their non-conformism, which is expressed through various behavioural manifestations, from dress (the jeans and T-shirts that are part of youth's common heritage everywhere) to lifestyles that break with accepted norms.
- Membership of a group centred on some activity, whether sports (*fanaty*, or team supporters), music (rockers), theatre, etc. Alongside the violent groups one finds 'pacifists' (Christians, Buddhists, etc.), 'ecologists' (Flora, Greens), or elitist groups whose inspiration is spiritualist (Systema).

Each group has its distinctive signs (Spartak football club's supporters wear scarves in the club's colors; the 'metalists' wear studded belts), its own leader, its special vocabulary, its enemies. This explains a measure of nomadism, expressed in an open preference for the street as opposed to home life, and for frequent job changes. These young people make up a whole community living on the fringes of the educational or industrial systems, whose hierarchic mode of organization has no room for young people in their decision-making processes. Because these young people are so rootless, they are sometimes prone to delinquency, prostitution, and drug addiction.[66] Of the 46,000 known drug addicts in 1986, 80 per cent were aged under thirty.[67] Here too, drug addiction leads to delinquency, a favoured form being car thefts, to sell off the spare parts, which are in short supply. But there are other, less pernicious means of escape available, and some turn to Yoga and other forms of esoteric Eastern philosophy or religious thought. An attraction even more powerful than the appeal of what is taboo, though, is the thrill of listening to their favourite bards. A veritable cult has grown up around certain officially frowned-upon poets such as Bulat Okudzhava or Vladimir Vyssotsky, who have given expression to the inner thoughts of these young people and to their chief demand, which is to be allowed to be themselves. This iconoclastic generation has yet to speak up, but what is going to happen when the time comes for it to take over?

It is not easy for the authorities to prevent these groups from proliferating.[68] Faced with a powerful craze like rock music, they have had to give some ground, granting permission provided the group is 'sponsored', i.e. financed by the Komsomol; that way they can exert some control over the repertoire. Young people chafe at this supervision. They shun organized leisure activities and want to choose their leaders themselves. Some of these young people claim to be fighting 'embourgeoisement' and 'conspicuous consumption' as they attack the Moscow cafés frequented by their better-off peers, relieving them of their Adidas sneakers in the process. Hooliganism has thus found an ideological pretext for its cult of force.

Soviet sociologists disagree as to the explanation for the popularity of rock culture. Some attribute the fights that break out between rockers and the *lyubery* (named after a Moscow suburb) to a class struggle between the privileged Moscow-dwellers, who enjoy not only higher incomes but also less social control, and the less well-off suburban boys. Others stress the effects of the crisis in the family and the absence of the father, which drives young people to seek a substitute authority, and the ethical void which leads to religion or the discovery of an absolute such as Love. In other words, rock has ceased to be an aesthetic issue and has become one of religion.[69]

Is this to say that the young are not interested in politics? Not at all: simply that they are mainly concerned with a handful of sensitive issues that do not always coincide with the goals of reform. For instance, young people bitterly resent inequality of opportunity in higher education

— hence access to good jobs in the future — which they feel to be an intolerable injustice. Everything that is now being done to regulate admission to the prestige schools to which the leadership's children used to enjoy privileged access — a telephone call used to be a more effective path to admission than knowledge — is welcomed. On the other hand, the *numerus clausus,* which is still in force and has even been strengthened, runs counter to the aspirations of the greatest number. Those who have failed to make it through the highly selective competitive examinations are, like increasing numbers of high school graduates, forced to find work in the factories, and their sense of frustration is hardly conducive to greater discipline in the workplace. According to foreign eyewitnesses, small groups of young students have formed to 'agitate' the working class and dispel its apathy as a means of supporting perestroika.

For those who do make it through the competitive exams, their study grants are no longer sufficient for their upkeep; formerly, if their families were unable to help them, they paid their way by all kinds of parallel activities. In Moscow, students used to have the monopoly of theatre ticket sales; they were divided into groups specializing in a particular theatre; others engaged in the more lucrative foreign-garments trade. A survey of teenagers has shown them to be thoroughly familiar with the different money-making schemes, and they knew the prices of brand-name goods.[70] The legalization of certain individual activities and the tightening of controls on black-market dealing have come as a blow to all those who used to eke out a living from unofficial activities. However, students, like pensioners, have been allowed to engage in sideline activities similar to those engaged in by students in the West.

There is one aspect of Soviet foreign policy to which young people today cannot be indifferent, and that is the war in Afghanistan. Conscripts are unenthusiastic. They have misgivings about this war 'where we've gone to de-

fend a cause that's none of our business'.[71] Discussion of
this war was long taboo, but now it has come out in the
open. *Pravda* condemned the prohibition on publishing
death notices (the war claimed some 2,000 per year);[72] and
on 19 August 1987, a TV talk show was devoted to the
difficulties encountered by the occupying forces. Hardly
surprisingly, many young men seek exemption from military service.[73] For the sake of fairness, the army mobilized
freshman and sophomore students, who had until then
been granted deferrals; however, this raised a storm among
the intelligentsia, who protested that this interruption of
studies would be 'prejudicial to the training of cultivated
people'.[74] The biting reply of the deputy chief of the general staff showed that there is plainly a cultural gap between the intelligentsia and the military, even though both
belong to the same privileged strata of society.[75]

NATIONALIST OUTBREAKS

The writers most under threat are the non-Russian ones,
who are often accused of propagating nationalist aspirations under cover of historical works or novels dealing with
their peoples' past. The historical panorama drawn by the
Kirghiz writer Chinghiz Aitmatov in *I Dol'she Veka Dlit'sya
Den'* is unmistakably reminiscent of his ancestors' traditions of honour and freedom. Although people have generally lost interest in the intellectual skirmishes aroused by
nationalist susceptibilities,[76] outbreaks of violence can
occur over the defence of their language. Back in the
1960s, the policy of Russification – which sought to make
the Russian language compulsory in certain examinations,
or to impose it as the second national language – caused
protests that shook Armenia and Georgia.[77] The abolition
or reduction of national schools in certain republics (the
Ukraine, Estonia, Byelorussia, and Moldavia) was felt to be
an attack on parental freedom of choice. On top of that,
Russians have poured into certain republics, altering the

balance of nationalities. In Kazakhstan and Kirghizia, the native people are now in the minority (respectively 36 and 48 per cent of the population); Russians now represent 38 per cent and 40 per cent of the populations of Estonia and Latvia respectively.[78] In the Ukraine, the study of the Ukrainian language in Russian schools is now optional.[79] As S. Kunayev said, 'A people's strength is its language, and every Kazakh ought to feel duty bound to be proud of his language. Considering a concern for one's language to be a sign of national egotism: that's what I call Russification.'[80]

Glasnost has undeniably provided an outlet for feelings of resentment which, while not necessarily political in nature, such as demands concerning the environment, still end up touching on questions of relations between dominators and dominated. When Enisa Petersa, speaking to the writers' plenum, referred to the dangers to the ecological balance in Estonia posed by certain projects, what he was in fact calling for was national integrity.[81] After that, all it took was an occasion such as the anniversary of the 1939 signing of the Molotov-Ribbentrop pact to spark mass demonstrations in the capitals of all three Baltic republics, on 23 August 1987. For the first time, the news agency Tass reported the events, accusing Western radio of having stirred them up; but similar demonstrations had already taken place in Riga in December 1986 and June 1987, to commemorate the victims of Stalin's repression in 1941, and more demonstrations were held on 18 November 1987. Demonstrations broke out again in the Baltic republics in February, to mark the anniversaries of the independence of Lithuania (16 February 1918) and Estonia (24 February 1918), in spite of appeals for calm by certain intellectuals.

In Alma-Ata, the capital of Kazakhstan, it was the recent purges – the sacking of Party secretary Dinmukhamed Kunayev and his replacement by a Russian, Gennady Kolbin, to head the Republic – that sparked a wave of violence killing two and injuring some two hundred people on 17 and 18 December 1986. However, the appointment of a Russian to head the Kazakhstan Communist Party is probably not the only explanation, in view of the fact that Russian secretaries such as Leonid Brezhnev have been appointed without incident in the past. Presumably significant, in addition to factors such as the feeling of power stemming from the rise of the Kazakhs, who currently dominate the Russians in twelve provinces out of nineteen, is the contagious example of the Afghan resistance. The demonstrators, most of them students, shouted 'Kazakhstan for the Kazakhs', then set upon Russian passersby, smashing shopwindows and setting fire to cars. The leader, a student, was sentenced to death. These events could scarcely go unnoticed in the neighbouring republics.[82] Among the Muslim peoples, the sense of community still runs strong, in spite of the secularization of society. There is no opposition between the egalitarian and populist ideals of Islam and those of communism; so much so that certain communist notables continue to observe the rituals of their religion.[83] The Soviet orientalist reporting these facts did not rule out the possibility that the troubles in Alma-Ata may have been influenced by fundamentalists outside the USSR, whose voices reach the Soviet Union via the Middle Eastern radio stations. He drew attention too to their influence on the Sufi sects, which form a widely ramified network of 1,800 unofficial mosques in Central Asia, Azerbaijan, and the Urals.[84] In Turkmenistan, the tombs of Afghan war deserters have become places of pilgrimage, and the kolkhozes have paid to build hardtop roads to visit them. The Afghan *mujaheddin* even claim to have raided the border regions of the Soviet Union with help from the Uzbek and Tadzhik populations. In Tadzhikistan, the first secretary of the Communist Party revealed at the Central Committee plenum of April 1987 that disturbances had

broken out at Kurgan-Tyube on the occasion of the trial of
a highly popular Muslim preacher, Sheikh Abdullah Sai-
dov, who was working to bring about an Islamic state along
Iranian lines. As in the past, Islam is proving to be a more
powerful unifying factor than communism in these regions,
which accounts for Gorbachev's diatribe against the sur-
vival of religious belief during his visit to Tashkent in
1987.

Among the Muslim nationalities, the Tatars, which were
the most numerous population under the old regime, have
never succeeded in creating a sizable political unit, owing
to their dispersal; the Soviet authorities have played upon
this division. The Crimean Tatars represented a community of over 200,000 before the war; in 1944 Stalin deported them to Central Asia to punish them because some
of them had collaborated with the German troops. Although they were rehabilitated in 1967, these Tatars were
never permitted to restore their republic, nor even to return to the Crimea, despite widespread protests.[85] The
most recent demonstration was in late July 1987, when
three hundred Tatars assembled in Red Square before the
gathering was broken up. A special commission was set up
under Gromyko to examine their demands. It is possible
that a small minority may be authorized to return to the
Crimea, where some of them have already resettled
clandestinely.[86] But it is highly unlikely that the Autonomous Region of the Crimean Tatars will be re-established,
as this would create conflict with the Ukraine, which was
given this territory in 1954. Plainly, the Kremlin is unwilling to jar the susceptibilities of the Ukrainians, lest their
latent nationalism be aroused.[87]

The Germans formerly had an autonomous district in
the Volga valley, and they too are in the same situation as
the Crimean Tatars. But many of them would rather emigrate to West Germany than demand their return to the
Volga. Already, 120,000 of them have left the country

under agreements with the Federal Republic of Germany.[88]

Jewish emigration from the USSR has resumed, although not at the levels of the 1970s: 51,000 people left in 1979, only 1,000 in 1986, and back to 13,000 for the first seven months of 1987.[89] The Soviet authorities would clearly like to be able to tie exit permits for refuseniks to Israel's agreeing to hold an international conference on the Middle East. The Kremlin would also like to confine this Jewish emigration to the reuniting of families provided for in the Helsinki agreements, which would rule out applications from anyone who cannot produce an invitation from a father, mother, brother, or sister living abroad.[90]

Of all the social problems for which it is impossible to foresee solutions even in the long term, the problem of the nationalities is surely the most explosive. As the writer Obzhosa Suleimenov acknowledges: 'The internationalist feeling which brought the nationalities together during the war has grown weaker under the impact of protectionism, localism [*mestnichestvo*]. . . . The idea of ethnic separatism knows no frontiers; words are its universal coin. We must never lose our sense of justice toward the nationalities. Although the question of the nationalities has been resolved, relations between nationalities, on the other hand, are still tense. In the present circumstances of swiftly developing democracy, we must expect to see a revival of centrifugal forces. The disease of nationalism may break out in any region.'[91]

In February 1988, Armenia provided a spectacular demonstration of this point by demanding the annexation of the autonomous mountain province of Karabakh (population 180,000, of which 80 per cent are of Armenian origin), which Stalin had given to Azerbaijan, a republic containing a majority of Shia Muslims, in 1923. The incidents that broke out at Stepanakert, the capital of this autonomous region, on February 13, spread to the capital of Armenia,

Yerevan, a few days later, attracting crowds of several thousands. Gorbachev despatched two envoys from the Politburo to restore order, but this did not prevent violence, which left several dead and injured at Karabakh and also caused injuries at Sumgait in Azerbaijan, in clashes between Armenians and Azeris.

For the time being, the central government has the situation well in hand, to judge from the extent of the purges that have been carried out in the outlying republics.[92] Moreover, to prevent demonstrations similar to those of the Crimean Tatars in Moscow, they are now subject to regulations.[93] These govern not only the non-Russian nationalities but also members of the Russian nationalist movement Pamyat, whose extremist positions cannot fail to be prejudicial to understanding between the peoples of the Soviet Union. How long would the Kremlin be able to confine manifestations of the different national cultures to folklore, and to keep 'attachment to the past from degenerating into attempted separatism',[94] if civil society were ever to regain its rights through 'democratization'?[95]

THE DISSIDENTS:
CHAMPIONING HUMAN RIGHTS

The word 'democracy' means different things even to people in Western Europe: for some it connotes a plurality of political parties and a free vote; for others, freedom of the press and education.[96] In a country like the Soviet Union, where none of these conditions obtains, the heralded 'democratization' obviously takes on a meaning different from the one given to it in the United Nations Charter of Human Rights. For those who have risked extreme harassment in pressing for human rights in the Soviet Union, the sole political support they have received for their moral dissidence has come from elsewhere. This has doomed them to impotence, for the inconsistency of the Western 'democracies' in their attitudes toward the USSR has tended to discredit the dissidents in the eyes of the Soviet man in the street, who regards them as spokespeople for foreign ideologies.

All the same, the Soviet leadership is not insensitive to the damage done to their image in the eyes of world opinion by their prosecution of dissidents. This led in early 1987 to the freeing of some 140 people who had been held in camps and whose cause had been taken up by the world press; they were granted their freedom on condition that they sign a statement promising to refrain from political activity from then on.[97] In January 1988, a large number of inmates were released from the psychiatric hospitals; at the same time, these hospitals were transferred from the Ministry of the Interior to the Ministry of Health.

The best known of the dissidents, Andrei Sakharov, who had been exiled to the city of Gorky since 1980, was allowed to return to Moscow in December 1986 and took part in the International Forum on Disarmament, where he spoke in favor of Gorbachev's initiatives. On 8 January 1988, during his first interview with Gorbachev, he handed him a list of 200 people imprisoned for their opinions while confirming his support: 'This kind of leader is needed in a great country at such a decisive moment in history.' He has, however, expressed his misgivings over domestic developments. The Soviet citizen's right to travel abroad continues to be strictly controlled, and Sakharov believes that freedom to emigrate should not be confined to the Jews alone but that there should be a law to deal with the substance of the issue. According to Sakharov, the process of consolidating the legal status of human rights is going to take years.[98]

The amnesty declared by the Supreme Soviet in 1987 to mark the seventieth anniversary of the Revolution, which covered mainly veterans and minors, did not apply to convictions under Section 70 of the penal code of the

RSFSR, which punishes 'propaganda designed to damage or weaken the Soviet authorities by the dissemination of defamatory writings or ideas'; Section 190–1, 'the verbal dissemination of calumnies'; Section 190–3, 'the organization of, and participation in, groups that disturb public order'; or Section 14 on the separation of church and state, which notably prohibits Bible meetings and religious instruction for children. According to Vladimir Lomeko, representative of the USSR on the United Nations Commission on Human Rights, there can be no question of amending these sections.[99]

The reform of the penal code and the procedural code is now in progress. Judicial practice will allow us to test the meaning of the word 'democratization' in the USSR. It is expected that indicted persons will be presumed innocent, which is not now the case in Soviet law. Also, it should be possible to bring a person's lawyer into the case right from the start of an inquiry – which is the case for underage delinquents – and not only at the end. At present, a person is charged by the state prosecutor, not by a judge, which means that the impartiality of the judicial system cannot be certain, since it is the prosecutor himself who is responsible for ensuring its impartiality.[100] A first step toward making prosecutors accountable was taken with the passage on 19 July 1987 of a law entitling citizens to sue civil servants for acting beyond their authority; this would cover prosecutors, who are state-appointed, unlike judges, who are elected. The law will not be retroactive, despite calls for compensation for past wrongs suffered by many citizens.[101]

The real problem is that of the judiciary's autonomy vis-à-vis the political authorities. The courts still have difficulty asserting this autonomy, being too frequently subject to pressure from the local authorities.[102] For the first time, the press has even carried reports of people being unjustly placed in mental hospitals.[103] Nonetheless the

jurists deserve credit; since Stalin's death they have cam-
paigned for the establishment of the rule of law. At their
urging, codes have been revised and laws have been passed
reflecting their expertise. The legal profession has gradually come 'to make decisions that are no longer subject to
political influence, displaying what must be accounted rare
independence in the Soviet context'.[104] Even so, the general prosecutor (procurator), unlike the US Supreme Court,
cannot rule on the constitutionality of decisions of the
political authorities, thus defending the rights of individuals where they conflict with what the authorities deem the
collective interest.[105] In a democratic society, the law is the
citizen's sole protector against the abuses of the state.
Soviet citizens are perfectly aware that glasnost could rebound on them if the law fails to guarantee that the change
is irreversible.[106]

CHURCHES AND BELIEVERS
The finest jurisprudence will not safeguard the quality of
justice if there are no moral principles to underpin the law.
In every society, morality has its roots in religious tradition, which is why religious conviction impels those who
fight to defend human rights.

Legally speaking, religious freedom is guaranteed by the
Constitution. But in practice, those with connections to
officialdom – schoolchildren and students, and civil servants especially – who display their religious convictions
or practice religion openly are liable to get into trouble
with the authorities. In towns where only one church is
open, they cannot hope to pass unnoticed; they therefore
prefer the anonymity of a big city.[107] An antireligious
drive in the 1960s considerably reduced the number of
places of worship open to the public: in the province of
Poltava, only 52 churches remained active in 1965, compared with 340 in 1960.[108]

There has been no change in the attitude of the authorities to the churches so far,[109] apart from minor relaxations such as the lifting of the order obliging priests to ask parents wishing to baptize their child, or young couples getting married, to show their passports. The law now allows religious communities to acquire property, and the Monastery of Saint Daniil in Moscow has been handed back to the Patriarchate of the Orthodox Church, after having been restored. The Kremlin has put out feelers to certain religious figures, although without implying any ideological concessions. The official celebration in 1988 of the thousandth anniversary of the Christianization of Rus (the name then used for the area comprising the present Ukraine, Byelorussia, and Russia) will represent a step along the road to recognition of the cultural role played by the church in the history of the country.[110]

The state professes a philosophy that is critical of religion and jealous of any authority liable to threaten its sovereignty, especially of religions whose centres are outside the USSR, as is the case for Jews, Baptists (suspected of having links to the United States), and Catholics. The Vatican has never recognized the annexation of Lithuania by the Soviet Union, and the Kremlin is using this as a pretext to refuse to allow the Pope to visit that republic, where, as in Poland, nationalism and religion are closely linked.[111]

One of the dignitaries of the Orthodox Church, the Metropolitan Alexis of Leningrad, has called in an official publication for glasnost to serve as an occasion for a change in the practice of relations between church and state, and he has invited the authorities to engage in dialogue so that believers will no longer be regarded as second-class citizens.[112] Recently released religious dissidents such as Father Gleb Yakunin have called for this also, in a letter to the Patriarch Pimen: 'The provisions of the 8 April 1929 act prohibiting the church from intervening in social life are still in force. Prayer, and in some cases preaching, are the only activities permitted. Preaching can never replace the school; systematic religious instruction is forbidden, as are Bible study circles or meetings of children, young people, or women for prayer. The sole freedom that it enjoys for the time being in the sphere of civil liberties is to proclaim that it – the church – is not suffering persecution.'[113] The hierarchy has dismissed these accusations as 'rash', on the grounds that realism and gradualism are needed in order to secure the revision of instructions contrary to the Constitution.

The demands of religious activists come from all the communities in the Soviet Union: Jews, Muslims, disciples of Hare Krishna, Christians. In letters dated 27 May and 11 September 1987, they call upon Gorbachev to revise the legislation on worship in the USSR, pointing out that as the thousandth anniversary of the conversion to Christianity draws near, believers ought not to be excluded from the process of democratization or marginalized. They also want venerated icons, currently in museums, to be returned to the churches. Some of these activists are trying to broaden public awareness. Two samizdat periodicals were presented to the Western press in July 1987. The first, the *Bulletin of the Christian Community,* published by A. Ogorodnikov, is common to all denominations, while the second, *Glasnost,* published by S. Grigoryants, is wider in appeal, containing information on all human-rights-related issues in the Soviet Union. The police are keeping a close watch on both, and they use what are called 'anti-Soviet articles' as a pretext for stepping in.

These isolated examples can hope to exert some influence only if they succeed in awakening some echo in public opinion. But as in other secularized societies, religious observance is declining in the USSR, averaging about 12 to 20 per cent in regions having an Orthodox tradition,[114] rising to 60 per cent in the Islamic regions. With the closing of the rural churches and the flight to the towns, the centre of gravity of religious observance has shifted to the urban areas, which is bringing with it qualitative changes. A greater number of men and young people now attend church, and the cultural level of practicing Christians is no lower than that of nonbelievers. It is no longer possible to regard belief as a form of obscurantism,[115] nor is hostility to believers as prevalent as it once was. Many believers are 'neophytes', with no family tradition of religious observance.[116]

In a country where religious traditions represent an inalienable part of the identity of the different nationalities, and in spite of the atheist education given in school, the popular consciousness still draws its moral bearings from often unconscious sources. They come to the fore in all recent debates on problems of values. Although they have been reduced to silence for ten years now and seemed to have failed in the political sphere, the dissidents had in reality set these debates in motion, imparting a moral content to present-day Soviet culture.[117]

4
.

THE GREAT DEBATE

.

■ The intellectual has replaced the cleric in propounding the values that gradually, at the propitious moment, build a new consensus and push society in new directions, as happened in Russia in 1861, 1905, and 1917. Today, too, the intelligentsia continue to inspire the deeper currents that are agitating Soviet society. That is why big debates that have so far been overlooked by the world's press probably foreshadow changes that could prove to be more important in the long term than those that have been observed in the very short run.

Whenever people have been permitted to debate ideas in the USSR, especially in the 1920s, two different views of Marxism have fought to gain the upper hand: a militaristic Leninism and a more humanistic doctrine. The current struggle over ideas is far more open than the political battle between the conservatives and the reformers. What makes it so distinctive is that it goes beyond some of the favoured dogmas of the past, such as the intrinsic virtues of centralized planning, the infallibility of the Party leadership, or the possibility of creating a 'new man'. 'For decades, the economic, political, and social sciences have laboured in the scholastic straitjacket of dogma, living in fear of purists indoctrinated with simple truths some thirty or fifty years beforehand. Are dubious, outdated dogmas to be allowed to thwart perestroika?'[1] The 'reformist' label used to be synonymous with deviationism or heresy; today it has become the rallying cry for all who 'want to progress'.[2]

The generation of intellectuals trained in the classical disciplines, who now find themselves calling for a return to traditional humanist values, are coming under attack from two quarters: the dogmatics accuse them of endangering the Party's leading role and paving the way for the restoration of bourgeois ideology; but they are also coming under attack from the representatives of the counterculture, who are idolized by youth and who are skilled in manipulating TV shows to their advantage and imposing the stereotypes of Western mass culture.

ECONOMIC STRATEGY AND SOCIAL GOALS

For the past thirty years or so, Soviet governments have looked to technology to solve their economic difficulties, without questioning the system itself. The panacea has been sought in turn in the chemical industry, automation and computers, and robots. Today, Soviet thinking is turning to the ends and means of development, to the need to take the 'human factor' into account and, consequently, the moral dimension of such issues.

This is not the first time that development strategy has been debated. The preparation of a textbook on socialist economics, as a pendant to the *Complete History of the CPSU* in the Classics of Marxism-Leninism series, was a focus of controversy for some ten years, until 1952, when Stalin decided that the law of value had no part to play in the shaping of the Soviet economy.[3] The 'fetishists of the law of value' were condemned for having compromised with the 'market' economy. The five-year plan was to be the sole point of reference. In vain did economists again argue in the 1960s that prices and other economic indicators (e.g. costs and profit) should be given a more central role.[4] Today, the problem of interdependence between plan and market continues to set the 'anti-commodity' group (whom their adversaries have nicknamed the 'cavalry', referring to their economic voluntarism) against the '*kuptsy*' clan (named for the merchant class under the old regime), who call for a marriage of planned economy and market.[5]

The latter are bitingly critical of the plan, which the Soviet system treats as a true *deus ex machina*. As Bonzhursky says in a 1987 *Literaturnaya Gazeta* roundtable, Gosplan has failed in its task through its inability to foresee major technological turning points like computers, letting the economy slip increasingly behind in technological terms and allowing sizable monetary imbalances to build up.[6] Similarly, the central-government ministries have proved incapable of supplying enterprises with ideas: all they can produce is an avalanche of paper.[7] In the roundtable, N. Petrakov points out, 'If Gosplan exists, that does not mean that the economy is obeying a plan. What functions according to plan in our country?' And Levikov adds, 'We have lived for many years surrounded by myths. We have ratified plans, but they have never been laws.' Lisichkin objects, 'We hold conferences on economic theory [*khozyashchet*], but we never put it into effect. We don't have any mechanism for selecting objectives, or rather, we set them by looking at the hats the bourgeoisie are wearing. We want to catch up with them without having the cadres and the technology, i.e. the necessary conditions.'[8] Pavlova-Silvanskaya has said, 'By denying the existence of contradictions, socialism has led us into bureaucratic utopia instead of pointing us toward the best. A tiny part of our plans has been fulfilled, because life couldn't care less about our plans.'[9] Petrakov adds, 'The remedy lies in a radical form, not directives but a living force; the market is that force. We must have the courage to become part of

the world market and to make the ruble convertible, which
will entail accepting a transitional period and a freeze on
living standards.'[10]

What the conservatives fear most is the social effect of
radical reform, on employment especially; whereas its advocates, on the other hand, think that a certain pool of
unemployment is bound to boost productivity.[11] They
argue for a break from the idea, as Lisichkin puts it, that
'society will look after you, come what may. To think that
way is not socialism but feudalism. In exchange for work
and security, the serf is bound body and soul to his lord.
The state takes care of the muzhik's health, dressing him,
housing him and feeding him. Socialism is the communal
food bowl, a hangover from feudal consciousness.'[12] 'In
our country, people live better than they work,' says A.
Zlobin in the roundtable; and Levikov adds, 'People claim
that state ownership transforms the individual by creative
collective involvement, that wage labour has been abolished, which is untrue as long as the individual receives
orders and as others decide for him.'[13] The workers' collective has been turned into an icon, and people kneel down
before it. 'One should see how the workers behave. Here
is an assembly line in a mechanical engineering factory.
The parts are there, but everyone's waiting for the last ten
days of the month before getting down to work so as to
work twelve hours a day and pocket 700 rubles. If the
manager responsible for fulfilling the plan remonstrates,
they boldly reply: Don't worry, we'll kick you out like the
last one.'[14]

Those who advocate liberalization of the economy, calling for an end to *uravnilovka* (the practice of redistributing
the profits of efficient enterprises to shaky firms via the
ministries, so as to ensure equal incomes for all), have a
tough job ahead of them to overcome egalitarian conceptions of socialism. Inside the enterprises, people acknowledge the damage done by *uravnilovka,* as it tends to

discourage effort by rewarding laziness,[15] but nobody is willing to step on his workmate's toes.[16] When workers are questioned about their earnings, those making less than 111 rubles overstate their real pay, and those making over 225 rubles understate it.[17]

Popular feeling remains hostile to individual enrichment (*chastnyi*) and work. The sole justification for enrichment is backbreaking labour[18] or accredited social function; for fear of being accused of illicit trading, a motorist will refuse to give an old lady a ride. Accordingly, the statutory instrument of November 1986 legalizing certain individual and co-operative activities really upset the applecart; a typical response was, 'Where are they taking us?'[19] Opponents have stressed the danger that labour would quit the state sector for the co-operative sector; there is talk of a return to the NEP and widening social inequalities. Encouraging individual enrichment is said to be contrary to the spirit of socialism, which is supposed to seek collective enrichment.

In reply, those who favor radical reform quote Lenin's writings at the time of the NEP justifying his political realism.[20] There is more genuine worker involvement in management in the co-operative sector.[21] Productivity gains and wages are higher in autonomous work teams. The way to attack the causes of shortages is by giving workers a share in the fruits of their labours. This assumes a linkage between earnings and work performed, provided the price system correctly expresses these relationships through the market. In any case, authorized enrichment will continue to be controlled by taxation, and the progressive income tax will skim off any surplus.[22]

Adversaries of bureaucracy are having to fight a widespread popular prejudice that the state embodies a superhuman force capable of putting everything to rights. All one need do is to extend its powers to those sectors that remain outside its control to overcome the negative effects of malfunctioning in the economy. Meddlesome control, they feel, is more effective than spontaneous processes.

Behind this debate over economic methods there looms a conflict between different sections of society, each having its own conception of social justice. This is apparent as soon as one touches on the question of inheritance. Those who defend this institution argue that parents have a natural desire to pass on to their children their social status, by giving them a suitable education. In the eyes of its opponents, who may have been less favoured in life, this is the epitome of injustice. How can they sit back and watch their children having to compete with fellow students whose parents can afford special tuition at 600 rubles a month to prepare them for competitive admission to the top schools? A worker who earns 200 rubles a month and saves only half of it would need to work ten years to buy a Zhiguli automobile.[23] Meanwhile, some people have amassed large enough fortunes to be able to live on their investments without working.[24] Some children come to view their position as not being the counterpart of their parents' labours and reproach them for not knowing how to live. Seen thus, inheritance serves merely to perpetuate social inequalities. The gap between rich and poor cannot fail to widen, as the cost of living increases by 3 per cent annually, and those who make their living by illicit trade continue to grow rich, while 40 per cent of households in the USSR have per capita incomes of less than 100 rubles a month.[25]

Between those who advocate efficiency and faster economic reform, and those who call for transitional measures in the name of social justice, there are divergent interpretations of socialism. Thus the concept has ceased to operate as a guide to consensual policy-making. So far, agreement has been reached only on palliatives. We may view this as evidence of the growing role of the bourgeoisie, which argues that enrichment is justified, as did the Protestants at the birth of capitalism.[26] One may also see it as a remnant of the traditional Russian peasant *mir*, where inequalities were corrected by periodical redistributions of common lands, or the tradition of the *artel*, in which collective earnings were shared out on the basis of each member's family situation. Even today in working-class communities, the predominant feeling is that 'we should move forward in step, not out of step'. Lisichkin claims to see in this a Christian reflex: that of sharing among members of a community, which people try to pass off as Marxism.[27] 'In Russia, the peasant is accustomed to collectivism, to the *obshchina* (rural community); he has it in the blood.'[28]

THE COMMUNITY AND NATIONAL HISTORY

Surely it seems paradoxical to refer here to peasant communities when these were destroyed by collectivization, and when most citydwellers have discarded community values for the lures of consumerism (*veshchizm*). These peasant virtues have ceased to exist in all but the imaginary world of the village prose-writers (*derevenskaya proza*), who have been portraying their gradual erosion for the past thirty years. Fedor Abramov was one of the first to sound the alarm and draw attention to the slow disappearance of traditional civilization: 'We are witnessing the last days of the old countryside; we are seeking with meticulous attention to pierce the secret of the type of man that it had created, to pierce the secret of our fathers and our mothers, the secret of our grandparents. . . . We have looked down upon them as an inferior breed, yet it is on their shoulders, on the shoulders of those labourers, of those unknown warriors, that the edifice of our present-day society rests. . . . Yes, they have little education and are extraordinarily credulous; they often lack education, but what hearts of gold they have, such radiance: infinite abnegation, an acute Russian consciousness, a love of the land and of all that lives. . . . Surely the time has come to raise the issue of the preservation and safeguarding of the permanent interests of our spiritual culture.'[29] Here is the author V. Belov on the condescending attitude that today's rural notables have inherited from their former masters: 'For them, the terms kolkhoz and village (*derevnya*) are synonymous with obscurantism. They think they know where the peasant ought to live, how he ought to dress, how he ought to sow.'[30]

Collectivization has removed all responsibility from the peasant. It is no longer the rank-and-file of the community that decides, as in the days of the *mir,* but an administrator who dictates instructions in line with unrealistic general directives, which in turn generate misleading reports and falsified farm-delivery records, which undermine people's moral sense.[31] Someone who himself steals is bound to turn a blind eye to theft by others. The myth of collective responsibility was derived from collective ownership; unfortunately, this collective responsibility has killed off individual responsibility.[32] Will the organization of work into autonomous teams (*bez naryad*) succeed in changing the peasant-turned-agricultural-worker into a civilized co-operative member? Ivan Vasiliev, a fine observer of rural life, thinks that only a small minority has any business sense (*delovitost*). The great majority of peasants just want to be left in peace.[33] The community has ceased to exist.

The writer V. Rasputin has illustrated this withering of the sense of community in a short story, 'The Fire' ('Pozhar'), in which he portrays the reactions of different people when fire destroys the storehouse in a Siberian village and all the provisions inside it. He contrasts the automatic mutual help and solidarity of the older, locally born generation (*korenniye*) with the attitude of the rootless workers (*letuchny*) who knock around Siberia and whose sole concern is to take advantage of the fire to pillage.[34]

The contemporary citydweller is rootless, alienated in the urban setting in which he lives confined; meanwhile in the countryside one no longer hears children's voices in the villages.[35] From nostalgia for the community to a critique of industrial civilization is but a short step. Belov attacks the idols of consumer goods (jeans and Pepsi-Cola), aggressive technology, the industrial system.[36] 'Manual labour is the only natural work for man.'[37] The craftsman in full possession of his craft had the spiritual satisfaction of the beauty of what he created. 'What has always saved Russia is not bunkers, but the Russian *izba*.'[38] The debasement of the values inherited from the past is bound up also with the crisis in the family. Belov makes no secret of his loathing of the liberated, wanton women who don't want children. He condemns the harmful influence of the West: you have to choose between Bach and rock music, between a love of history and sex.[39]

The nineteenth-century Slavophiles would not have disclaimed this profession of faith, but it is far from being universally approved; it has been considered provocative, even antisemitic.[40] Officially, this type of literature has long been denounced as passé and reactionary. Today, though, the 'Great Russian' nationalist ideal is finding support among the military. The populist ideals of another age are surfacing again. 'The people are the incarnation of social, national, and historical justice,' proclaims S. Zalygin, as he casts about for a means to revive the sense of community without which there can be no collectivism.[41] For him, there can be no morality without something to tie the people to their past; present-day realities cannot be separated from those of yesterday: 'Our life does not begin on the day we are born, but on the day our mother is born.'

'The history they teach us is sociology without the actors,' writes one critic. 'They have dehumanized history [*obezlyudili*], or else the hierarchs of antiquity are presented like figures from de Maupassant, so as to strengthen the atheism of our contemporaries. A civil servant arrogates to himself the right to change the names of towns that have been there for hundreds of years.[42] A politician who thinks history began when he came to power does not inspire optimism [does he have anyone in particular in mind?]. People just want to live from day to day [*odnodnev-nye lyudi*] and think that that is a sign of wisdom. Without a knowledge of history, one cannot build a new life.'[43] Another observes, 'People are ashamed of the way history, literature, and philosophy are taught. Whole sections have been wiped out. Visitors to the Hermitage are incapable of understanding a masterpiece such as Rembrandt's *Return of the Prodigal Son,* because they have never read the Bible. And how can they hope to understand the legend of the Grand Inquisitor, one of the most sublime moments in world literature? . . . Tenth-grade children have never learned anything but the history of the socialist countries, and are ignorant of the history of the countries we have fought against. They ought to reissue a classic like *The History of the Russian State* by Karamzin, and among the nineteenth- and twentieth-century Russian idealist philoso-phers, people like Vladimir Soloviev and others.'[44] 'Major periods in our history have become untouchable; one could not publish anything on them, as if one could slice up history and retain only its bright side. We must open the doors.'[45]

These recommendations raise awkward questions – such as the role played by Lenin's colleagues, who have been expunged from the textbooks, or the period of collectiviza-tion and the purges of 1936–38 – that can be answered only by those in authority. But even before any such deci-sions had been made, a new wind began to blow, with publications and plays dealing with historical themes: the plays of Mikhail Shatrov (*Dictatorship of the Heart; The Brest Peace*), Anatoly Rybakov's novel *Children of Arbat* (written in 1966, scheduled for publication in 1968, finally published in April 1987), Tenghiz Abuladze's film *Repent-*

ance, novels dealing with the gruesome episodes of the Stalin era, such as those by Boris Mozhayev and Daniil Granin.[46] There have been groundbreaking articles on history, as in the special issue of *Pravda* on the collectivization and the article in *Ogonek* dealing with the purges.[47]

In regard to these past events, inside the Politburo there have been subtle differences between the statements of Gorbachev and those of Ligachev before the festivities marking the seventieth anniversary of the October Revolution.[48] The speeches made for the anniversary itself reflected the consensus finally arrived at in the Politburo, together with the limits to permissible revision. While Bukharin is now acknowledged to be a 'valuable theoretician, he must be handled carefully', because 'he underestimated the strength of the time factor in the construction of socialism'.[49] Trotsky, on the other hand, remains the archvillain, 'with his exaggerated claims, shifty and dishonest, hoping to foment a split within the Party'. Stalin 'was responsible for the triumph of Leninism'. He is credited with having industrialized the country and for his role in World War II. However, 'The guilt of Stalin and his immediate entourage before the Party and the people for the wholesale repressive measures and acts of lawlessness is enormous and unforgivable. This is a lesson for all generations.'[50]

Gorbachev has dwelt on the tragic history of collectivization at great length, acknowledging that the Party had 'not been attentive to the interests of the "middle" peasants, the majority of whom had supported the Revolution. If we had succeeded in striking an alliance with them against the kulaks, we would have avoided the excesses of collectivization.'[51] The administrative methods used at that time were then extended to the rest of the economy and 'to the superstructure acting as a break on the development of democracy'. Tribute has been paid to Khrushchev for his courage in criticizing 'the personality cult' and in restoring socialist legality. The process of rehabilitation initiated after the twentieth and twenty-second congresses was not carried to its conclusion; a special commission has been set up to establish the truth and restore justice on this period.[52] But it is out of the question to use this revision as a pretext for a series of trials to exact revenge: 'We are proud of each of the days that we have lived . . . , which is why we cannot countenance any show of disrespect to our people, to the generations that experienced all that and have brought our country to the present.'[53]

There is nothing iconoclastic in what Gorbachev has to say there. Although he does seek to fill in certain 'blank pages' in the history of the Soviet Union, he still leaves its greatest tragedy in the dark, namely the millions of dead: 'a sum that has never been reckoned'.[54] He also avoids recalling that part of the past that deals with the colonization by the Russians of the Caucasian and Central Asian peoples.[55] Gorbachev's portrayal of seventy years of Soviet history is faithful, on the whole, to the customary line, justifying the broad policies in the name of 'objective necessities'.

It might have been feared that Gorbachev was thus delineating a new historical orthodoxy. Some expressed alarm at the reasons he gave: 'The logic of the revolutionary struggle encapsulates everything that is contrary to the Revolution if it excludes the human factor from the struggle. It was a struggle for an idea, man being nothing but the illustration of that idea. They loved the sheer scale of their plans for the good of the people, and in that scale, man as a concrete being disappeared. Their logic was the following: he who is the enemy of the Soviet regime must be crushed. What is this policy which permits lies? We must struggle for the truth, for nothing but the truth. Attachment to principles is the death of man.'[56] Gorbachev replies, 'Understanding our history is not a matter that has been settled once and for all; it will become deeper and will

develop in the course of subsequent examination.'[57] The
October 1987 plenum gave the job of this 'examination' to
a specialist commission that was to publish some of its
findings in time for the Party conference in June 1988. The
debate is by no means over, since Gorbachev returned to
the theme at the 18 February 1988 plenum: 'The quest for
truth is no grounds for hasty judgements, which can only
lead to superficial conclusions.'

ELITISM AND
MORAL CONSCIOUSNESS

To recreate a community, though, it is not enough to restore the truth about the past; one must also create genuine
relationships among people. Life has withered because it
was thought that justice could be made to reign by authoritarian means. 'During the campaign against the kulaks,
relatives and neighbors were forbidden to come to the aid
of the families of victims. In the 1930s, compassion disappeared from our vocabulary. Lies insinuated themselves
into the family; they destroyed the spirit of solidarity, the
concern for other people.'[58] The claim to want 'to create
a new man is one of the stupidest tragedies of the twentieth
century.'[59]

Order is established not by fines and brickbats, but by
the centuries-old rules of the community.[60] The 'technical'
intelligentsia (in Western parlance, the technocracy) is incapable of recreating this community. For that, one needs
'an intelligent'.[61] This Russian term is not used lightly. It
serves to highlight the difference between this concept and
the official definition that places everyone with a higher
educational degree in the intelligentsia; it refers to the
period in the nineteenth century when idealistic intellectuals sought to spread socialism in the countryside. The
distinctive feature of these 'intelligents' was that culture
was their intellectual criterion, and consciousness their

moral criterion. They were the elite who would play a major role in the future Soviet society.

But how to form this elite, given the absence of 'cultivated' people?[62] Public opinion is hostile to any form of selection, but eminent scientists and academics invited to ponder the question have criticized the present educational system and come out in favour of selection in the twelfth grade of high school. This, they say, will obviate the need for tutoring to prepare for entrance to the advanced schools by competitive exam; moreover, they argue, it will prevent the special schools, to which admission used to be based on one's connections, from becoming 'schools for one class only' (*soslovie*).[63] Proposals have even been put forward for a special school employing co-operative methods, independently of the official curriculum, to train elite pupils from the secondary system.[64]

On the other hand, school can have only a limited influence on the moral education of children. According to V. Rozov, this aspect of education depends on the soundness of the family. It can be fully effective only if wages are calculated so that both parents are not obliged to work. But neither the family nor punishments nor rewards will be of any use in training a decent citizen unless the individual educates himself. This vision of 'self-education' is closer to the teachings of Tolstoy than to Marxism, which claims that the determining factor is the environment.[65]

Many writers also concur with Tolstoy in placing the heart of morality in the conscience.[66] The divided man, the dual personality – these terms recur time and time again, like a straitjacket from which one must escape before one can be free again.[67] 'We have grown accustomed to living a double life, to saying one thing and thinking another.' Out of fear, people have lacked civic sense. This moral conscience awakens in us a sense of honour – not to be confused with pride in membership of a caste (*chest' mundira*)[68] – and a sense of compassion. The man who will never act contrary to his conscience belongs to this elite of the moral conscience, whom Granin counterpoises to the elite of intelligence.[69]

What does all this talk of morality amount to, and how are people reacting to it?

First, we may see in it a propensity on the part of the intelligentsia to place its opposition to the regime on a moral ground, creating a solidarity of spirit with all those who wish to eschew politics. The reasons for their wavering attitude lies in 'fear, which continues to paralyze people's conscience'. Though the 'personality cult' has been condemned, glasnost can be no substitute for democracy: 'We must learn democracy and patience,' says D. S. Likhachev.[70] But this interpretation would run counter to Russian tradition, in which the intellectual is the spokesman for the conscience of society. The writer is not a Pontius Pilate; he still has a high idea of his moral obligations to the people.[71]

But that is just the point: the people are no longer willing to accept an elitist conception of culture. For the people, such a conception is further evidence (in line with justifications of getting rich) of the encroaching values of a bourgeoisie determined to confiscate from the people their sole gain from the Revolution – access to culture and social mobility. One worker has exclaimed, 'You want to create an elite cut off from the rest of society, which would reserve to itself the opportunities to learn music and foreign languages.'[72] Many view these appeals to the moral conscience as mere humbug: 'We all know what it costs to follow one's conscience, for oneself and one's family and friends'. No one can level this criticism at Likhachev, who has experienced prison and the tragedy of whole generations. Nor can it be leveled at Granin, who has become the defender of the humiliated and the injured of the Soviet society, of all the poor, of whom there are still many, who are never mentioned in literature, and of all those who have suffered from the injustices of the past, and the millions uprooted by war, occupation, and captivity.[73]

Others criticize this morality for reproducing the morality of the church. V. Bykov replies that religion merely preaches the human values of pity and compassion, which are universal.[74] Morality is innate to man.[75] The spiritual quest visible in the work of many authors[76] is therefore not necessarily synonymous with a return to religion, although one needs to beware of generalizations in so intimate a sphere. What is visible also is the rejection of all dogmas. This can be seen in the way the counterculture derides all forms of academicism and all values, whether imposed or proposed. There is a risk that this popular culture, with its mingled tears, laughter, and aggression, is going to attract a growing following as the rock culture comes to hold the key to admission to the youth tribe, although young people are capable of displaying generosity when some really important occasion arises.[77]

Looking for a common denominator to all these debates, we find that, apart from technical solutions of an economic nature, everything concerning values refers to tradition rather than to modernism. That is the price to be paid for decades of isolation and inward-looking concern on the part of the Soviets themselves; it is due also to the fact that the chief protagonists in these debates belong for the most part to the prewar generation. Little mention is made of Marxism-Leninism. Perhaps this is because socialist ideology and morality have been incapable of providing answers to existentialist questions. 'We thought there was nothing to look for because everything had been found; all one had to do was comment and criticize. Today, the Party condemns rigid opinions: we need to seek, to seek together.'[78] Depending on whether one is optimistic or pessimistic, one may view this unexpected outpouring of heterodox confessions and proposals as the awakening of a critical consciousness, rejecting dogmas after decades of serfdom, feudalism, and scholasticism, or as an interlude to 'let a hundred flowers bloom.' For notwithstanding the authenticity of the accounts cited above, the Agitprop officials are ever-vigilant, and they retain more or less visible control over everything that is published.

The man generally acknowledged to be the inventor of glasnost, Alexander Yakovlev, has himself spelled out the limits to the process.[79] On many points, what he says coincides with the moralists' arguments: 'The final essence of the reforms set in motion by the April 1985 plenum is the restoration of morality. . . . Life has painfully and obstinately brought home to us that political and economic successes are ephemeral, whereas man is eternal and his moral values imperishable. . . . Education in the meaning of the dignity of man is probably one of the most urgent tasks. It is inseparable from the notion of consciousness and the yearning for self-fulfillment, to fill one's life with spiritual content. . . . There is a need to put a revolutionary end to the practice whereby some people uttered imperious prophecies, while the rest listened docilely. The changes that have occurred demand that we shed dogmatic prejudices.' But he also makes clear what is forbidden: 'Mass culture that appeals to violence and gives vent to antisemitism, Zionism, nationalism, and chauvinism, which are liable to endanger the internationalism that is the cornerstone of Marxist-Leninist doctrine, by playing upon religious prejudice or exaltation of the feudal or bourgeois past.' The general in charge of political affairs in the Red Army has dotted the 'i': 'While we accept arms parity with the West, parity is out of the question in the cultural and moral sphere.'[80] Gorbachev has set the limits to discussion in a single sentence: 'Pluralism is acceptable solely within the framework of socialism, and everything that runs counter to socialism must be combatted.'[81]

5
■

PERSPECTIVES AND SOCIAL FORCES

■

■ To have any effect on society, the debate on values must be able to refer to some social forces. For the time being, the only organized force is the Party. Gorbachev's personal situation is of decisive importance. To strengthen it, he will have to come to an arrangement with the different tendencies represented inside the Politburo, which accounts for the stop-and-start tempo of the reforms. Nothing fundamentally irreversible has been done so far; implementation of the most significant changes has been delayed until after 1990. Five years from now, Gorbachev is bound to be judged on his economic record. He needs to be able to press on the accelerator in order to obtain tangible results, while proceeding with caution so as to overcome resistance to his policy.[1] We can, however, try to gain some of the necessary perspective, using broad policy directions and the forces of resistance and support for those policies to guide us.

The façade of the edifice of power looks imposing, being sustained by an awesome military and police machine; but this façade has begun to crumble in recent years, because the economic system has not been able to adapt quickly either to technical progress or to the needs of a more sophisticated population. Behind the appearance of hard-line centralism, the system of government has become compartmentalized into myriad and ramified feudal fiefs, which has added the spectacle of corruption to the inefficiency of bureaucracy. Restoring the authority of the state required economic reform and a purge of corrupt officials. But the fact that the Soviet institutions form a whole and cannot be reformed gradually, by degrees, makes it all the harder to achieve these objectives. Furthermore, those in charge of the operation are officials and administrators who enjoy all the advantages of the existing system. They are in no hurry to lose their privileges,[2] and the workers are unwilling to change their habits.[3]

What forces can Gorbachev count on in his battle with the hydra of bureaucracy? The purges initiated by Yuri Andropov had already gone some way to renewing the machine, but the recent replacements do not yet form the majority in the Central Committee. This accounts for differences of formulation between Gorbachev's statements and those of some of his colleagues, and the resolutions passed by plenums or the Party program adopted by the twenty-seventh congress. The Party conference, scheduled for 28 June 1988, is expected to strengthen the reformist clan.

Between now and then, Gorbachev has drawn support from those who enjoy some credit among the population and are therefore in a position to lead public opinion. It has been necessary to grant the intelligentsia greater freedom of expression and, in the process, to release certain dissidents belonging to this section of society. At the same time, Gorbachev has thrown the weight of the rank-and-file activists into the balance, so as to exert pressure on the bureaucracy in place, encouraging them with media assistance to bring out into the open – which is precisely what glasnost means – all that had been lurking in the shadows.

The bureaucratic phenomenon is not inherent to the

development of industrial society; indeed it is more in evidence in an underdeveloped state, where the administration more easily escapes control by those whom it is supposed to serve. An employee or civil servant may be called a bureaucrat when, in the performance of his duties, he feels that he can act with impunity, protected by his superiors, and that the public can do nothing about his attitude. Glasnost, far more so than extension of the electoral system, is a powerful weapon in bringing the administration back under the control of its users. It is only to be expected that the threat now hanging over civil servants should arouse not just concern but hostility.

This hostility arises at two levels: (1) the local and regional officials who act as a screen between the central government and the grass roots, and (2) sectional interests speaking for the various branches of the economy – including the powerful arms lobby – which are represented at the summit and are capable of calling in ideological arguments in support of their interests. This explains why the economic reform initiated by the new law on the enterprise has resulted in a compromise in which a series of state orders (*goszakazy*) has been put in place to safeguard the positions of the defenders of central planning. For the time being, the free-market sphere is confined to contracts between enterprises – once priority orders have been fulfilled; meanwhile, on the contrary, centralized control has expanded its sphere in the form of inspection by the state commission for control of the quality of manufactured goods (Gospriemka) at the time of acceptance, a procedure which formerly applied to the arms industry only. Agreement has been reached, finally, not to modify the current five-year plan so as not to imperil its fulfillment, hence the postponement until 1991 of the principal measures – price reviews and the introduction of a wholesale trade – that will lay the bases for the reform of the economic system.

Between now and then, top economic officials will have

to juggle wages and prices to avoid sudden changes liable to trigger tension, especially if the closing of unprofitable enterprises were to threaten jobs.

Perestroika is not being hampered by political obstacles alone; certain preconditions are required before the new system can be put in place. The present situation is reminiscent of the USSR in 1948, when the government had to abolish rationing and fix prices at an intermediate level between official prices and free-market prices. Subsidies on essential foods will most likely be phased out, rather than being abolished at a stroke, so as to prevent any sudden, sharp increase in retail prices (supposing it were possible to bring down the mass of inflationary liquidity in the economy). The most radical solution would be a monetary levy of the kind imposed in 1948. For the time being, enterprises are under pressure to hold down wages, since they are now expected to fund their expenditures out of revenues. Consequently it is no longer in their interest to hold on to excess personnel. This in turn raises the delicate problem of unemployment.

Nationwide, the Soviet Union suffers from labour shortages rather than surpluses. The population of working age will rise by 6 million workers between 1986 and 2000, allowing for people retiring, compared with an increase of 30 million between 1970 and 1985.[4] But the regional picture obviously differs from one city to another. In Moscow, industry and the services are short of manpower, whereas government offices are harder hit than elsewhere by perestroika. Until now, cuts in the personnel of two ministries, from 1,702 to 1,022 employees, have occurred without difficulty; as the first to go, the redundant workers were able to find vacant positions elsewhere. In certain cases, where the functions of government agencies devolve upon enterprises, the civil servants can be transferred to those enterprises. Matters are a good deal more complicated in the case of the big industrial concentrations of the

Donbas or Urals, where the labour exchanges have recently become inundated with job seekers. At Voroshilovgrad, 500,000 job applications were recorded in a single three-month period.[5] The republics of the Caucasus raise specific problems, owing to rapid population growth and stricter controls over the itinerant *artel*s of construction workers (*shabashniki*), who used to find lucrative seasonal work.[6] Aganbegyan does 'not believe that the closing of unprofitable enterprises is taking on a mass character'.[7] As always when the authorities are faced with labour conflicts, they tend to give in by devising a compromise solution. Rather than shut down the plant, the likeliest outcome will be staff cuts or job-saving changes in the product mix.

So far, notwithstanding a handful of sporadic strikes, the country has not experienced anything dramatic on a par with what has happened in Poland. The notion of pluralistic labour unions has not secured a foothold in workers' attitudes, and because the Party has always succeeded in turning to its own ends the characteristic desire for unity (*splochennost'*) found in the Russian peasant and working-class traditions; also, the vast expanse of the Soviet Union and the fact that it contains many different nationalities prevent the emergence of a broad labour movement. Most of the time, conflicts are settled on the shop floor, between the foreman and his team, as paternalism and sentiment prevail over their relations in the hierarchy. This calm could well be short-lived, because glasnost is making young people, who for the most part belong to the working class, far more arrogant; moreover, not only are these youths going through a transitional period between school and adult-worker status, but they have also become a social force to be reckoned with and which has interests of its own. Young people's immediate concerns are that the Afghan war poses a threat to their career and their very existence. Why should technocrats have the right to define the social needs in whose name selective entry to the ad-

vanced schools and career guidance determine their future? Why does Foreign Minister Shevardnadze spend so
much of his time traveling abroad when he ought to be
putting an end to the war in Afghanistan?[8]

These young people are perfectly capable of enthusiasti-
cally embracing a great cause, as events showed at Alma-
Ata in 1986, when students sparked off events that ended
in brutal repression. Certain demonstrations have been
tolerated, however, such as the ones instigated by the intelligentsia in defence of the national heritage and for the
conservation of natural resources[9] – in other words, essen-
tially conservative movements. These campaigns have
awakened a wide response in youth and attracted its support.[10] One can even speak of the emergence of civil society in this respect, as these movements have in certain
cases been powerful enough to modify official decisions. As
a result, for example, stricter controls have been imposed
on industrial pollution of Lake Baikal (statutory instrument of April 1987);[11] major waterway schemes such as
the plan to divert certain big rivers, which threatened to
upset the ecological balance of vast areas of the Soviet
Union, have been dropped (statutory instrument of 16
August 1986); and a grandiose projected monument to the
dead of World War II, which was to have been erected in
Moscow in the pompous style of the Stalin era, has been
shelved also.

It will presumably take quite some time before this
embryonic civil society is able to find expression in the
political sphere, owing to the authorities' fear of 'spontaneous' outbursts by 'unorganized' movements (i.e. outside the
Party). They would prefer to channel them into associations such as the National Cultural Fund or the Vladimir
Lenin Children's Fund. In September 1987, forty-seven
unofficial organizations, represented by six hundred delegates, held a symposium in Moscow (the first of its kind),
which concluded by drafting a common platform commit-

ting them to uphold the ideals of socialism and democracy. The platform also contained a fourfold rejection: of violence, of sectarianism (the monopoly of the truth), nationalism, and racism.[12]

Perceptible in the wording of these rejections is the concern to deter the ecology movements from rushing off to campaign against nuclear energy, now that public opinion, especially in the Ukraine after the Chernobyl accident, is sensitive to this danger.[13] Already science-fiction writers have reflected the widespread public concern over the dangers of nuclear power.[14] But from the defence of the environment one moves imperceptibly to the defence of the national community; in other words, it is hard to prevent the slide into nationalism. Hardly anyone needs reminding that in Czechoslovakia in 1968 it all started with economic reform and the easing of censorship in the media, and that it ended with demands for the right to self-determination and the subsequent entry of Soviet troops.

Recent events have shown that the USSR is not immune to outbreaks of violence arising out of conflicts between the nationalities. The Pamyat association of 'Great Russian' nationalists is not exactly designed to allay such sentiments.[15] Given the size of some of this movement's rallies – e.g. the one attended by almost a thousand people at the Dynamo Stadium in Moscow in 1987 – there are grounds for supposing that advocates of 'the Russian Idea', with its antisemitic overtones, enjoy support in the Party machine and in the army.[16] But Pamyat is a risky ally, owing to the hostility it arouses among the non-Russian minorities, among whom the nationalist demon is rearing its head also.[17] Now, all gatherings are subject to prior authorization, as a result of a recent government order;[18] but the regulation is powerless to prevent popular outbursts such as the one in Armenia in early 1988.

Nor can official doctrine on the national question provide a response to the fears of minorities under threat of

Russification. To state, as Gorbachev has, that 'our strength lies in the free development of national cultures. True internationalism is possible only if one has a profound respect for the dignity, honour, culture, and history of each people'[19] is to claim to reconcile two opposing conceptions of the nation, namely 'proletarian internationalism' and nationalism. The Bolsheviks had hoped that the communist ideology would prove a sufficiently powerful integrating factor to overcome national particularisms. As for the heirs to the Enlightenment, the nation consisted of a union of wills around a common social project; as for all revolutionaries, this conception overlooked the importance of the past and traditions. This ideology having failed – Stalin was obliged to revert to extolling Russia's past at the time of World War II – it has been replaced by a romantic vision of the nation founded on a community of traditions and the specific genius of the nation.

Given the patchwork of communities, this revival of the sense of national identity represents a break with the universalism – not to be confused with class struggle based on communist internationalism – which alone could transcend these conflicts.

It is plainly impossible to predict what is going to happen to the Soviet empire. The dynamics of population growth among the nationalities of the USSR is tending to whittle away the Russian predominance.[20] National cultures are constants in the lives of people; they have survived the modernization of society, as witnessed by the example of Japan. On the other hand, the now-inescapable modernization of the Soviet Union (which indeed it now wants to hasten) points up two major transformations. First, the trend is to growing professionalization, through the education needed to master the technologies of tomorrow.[21] Second, the country is opening up to the outside world, as these same modern communications technologies mean that states' frontiers can no longer isolate societies permanently from outside influences. The day Soviet citizens are free to travel to the country of their choice – which would be more effective in shaking the country out of its lethargy than any number of campaigns of socialist empathy – would signal the victory of competence and democracy over dogma.

We should not, however, underestimate the present phase, for it has set in motion a series of irreversible processes whose effects will be felt only in the long run. If, as D. S. Likhachev claims, 'people no longer want to be mere blinkered executants of some outside will',[22] the break (*perelom*) would be comparable to the one that occurred in the West on 31 October 1517 in Wittenberg, when Martin Luther proclaimed that man was answerable to no one but his own conscience. That set in motion the Reformation and the Renaissance.

It is impossible to measure the social consequences of such a break with the past, for moral progress is an individual affair, and it would be naïve to imagine that a society can achieve virtue by decree. But the law can be an effective safeguard against individual shortcomings. That is why the present policy of legalizing public acts represents a guarantee for the future against arbitrary government. Already, we are no longer able to keep track of the detailed circumstances of events: Yeltsin was removed from leadership of the Moscow Gorkom without public humiliation and in accordance with democratic procedures. Still more significant was Gorbachev's statement to representatives of the Soviet media on 8 January 1988: 'We are spared no criticism, from right or left. The latter claim that restructuring has come to a halt; they call for firm measures, for wholesale removal of cadres. . . . On the right, certain people even go so far as to accuse us of undermining the foundations of socialism.'[23] In contrast with the customary attacks on factions within the Party, this admission of the existence of different currents constitutes implicit recognition of pluralism. This step had to be taken inside the Party before it could gradually be extended to civil society. 'Today more than ever before, it is clear that the battle of ideas, the diversity of opinions, projects, experiences, and plans in every sphere of life without exception, is the prerequisite of efficiency, vitality, and dynamism. Wherever this pluralism is excluded artificially, by directives, stagnation is the inevitable outcome. Perestroika is only beginning; the problem is not to achieve everything all at once, but to ensure that we do not stop along the way at some time in the future.'[24]

It will probably take another generation or two before the spirit of the reforms so far begun and freedom of expression inside the Party filter through the masses. The time factor is part and parcel of change in and of society. This is not the first time in the history of Russia that a major reform – e.g. the abolition of serfdom in 1861 – has been initiated at the summit in the absence of democracy and contrary to the interests of the privileged sections of the nation, 'because the inefficiency of the economy and the progress of education were making the gulf between the ideals of freedom and equality and the reality of a regime based on serfdom ever more intolerable to the intelligentsia.' The great Russian historian V. D. Klyuchevsky, who described the reign of Alexander II in those terms, concluded on a note of cautious optimism: 'If we have not yet completed this adjustment [of reality to ideals], the generation that we have raised and which will follow, will do so in our place.'[25]

6

■

SECOND OPINION

■

■ This final chapter has its odd title because it was written six months after the rest of the book. The intervening events shed an interesting light on my earlier analysis. Rather than add to it or alter it, I have preferred to offer a revised overview, even at the risk of some repetition or rectification of my earlier judgements.

THE ISSUES AT STAKE AND THE REASONS FOR PERESTROIKA

Three years have passed since the Central Committee Plenum of April 1985, which set in train a whole series of changes at Mikhail Gorbachev's instigation. Today we are in a better position to assess the tenor and the limitations of those changes. The picture now emerging in its full complexity also reveals the logic underlying the decisions, and the resistance they are encountering.

The men who took over the controls of state and party from a series of senile gerontocrats had no illusions about the stagnant condition of the Soviet economy or the consequent political weakening of their country. Its accumulated handicaps put the USSR in growing danger of becoming a second-rank power. Just as defeat in the Crimean War convinced the tsar of the need to abolish serfdom (1861), so the desire to rise to external challenges precipitated the present set of reforms that we call perestroika: their purpose is to emancipate the economy and society from that more recent form of serfdom, the bureaucratic and totalitarian state instituted by Stalin.

This is not the first time since the last war that an effort has been made to stimulate the economy. But the economic reforms of Khrushchev in 1957, like those of Liberman and Kosygin in 1965, failed because they did not go to the root of the problem – namely the lack of sufficient incentives for the individual to feel he has a stake in his work.

Political reforms were needed to mobilize the 'human factor', for without freedom, workers merely pretend to take part. What they needed was an opportunity to speak up (glasnost), to denounce the failures and the squalid compromises of the system through the voice of the intelligentsia, which has served to catalyze embryonic public opinion.

This is a highly delicate undertaking, because people are not prepared mentally for the resulting revelations, and also because it involves nothing short of reforming institutions that have functioned for decades subject to no control other than the Party monopoly. Yet it is precisely this monopoly that is indirectly threatened by present attempts to marry centralized planning with free-market economics, and by the elements of pluralism that glasnost is introducing into the hitherto sacrosanct ideological sphere.

If the extent of these changes depended solely on the will and charisma of the man who had the courage to launch them, then we should not bank too heavily on Mikhail Gorbachev's chances of success. He is running into considerable resistance, even opposition. But time is on his side; objective factors make today's reforms a necessity.

The changes have not sprung up through spontaneous generation. They are in line with the logic underlying the process of modernization of Russian society that began well before the 1917 October Revolution. This process, which was heading naturally toward a free-market economy and parliamentary democracy, was stopped in its tracks by Lenin and Stalin, as they tried to speed up the action of the laws of history and usher in a classless society. As elsewhere, industrialization in the USSR has profoundly altered the social foundation of the country, turning a peasant nation into an urban, educated, and diversified society. But this functional diversification has not produced autonomy for the different spheres of social life in the Soviet Union, as it has in the West, although that autonomy is essential if they are to develop successfully. Economy, culture, and civil society have suffocated under the domination of a single Party that draws its sole legitimacy from a totalitarian ideology.

What is being played out today is determining the future of the uncompleted modernization of the Soviet Union. That does not mean a conversion to capitalism, which is merely a now-superseded phase in the development of industrial societies. What it does signify is the possibility for the economy, scientific research, education, artistic creation, and freedom of conscience to develop in accordance with their own internal demands: and that implies legal guarantees to safeguard the rights of the individual. The separation of powers and the rule of law have long been the failsafe mechanisms that have enabled Western societies to innovate in the technical sphere while broadening the scope of social welfare. The theses designed to institute a state based on the rule of law, which were submitted to the Party conference on 28 June 1988, therefore represent a major milestone in the history of the Soviet Union.

Like all far-reaching reforms, this one is unwelcome both to the beneficiaries of the regime – the privileged members of the machine, who administer their bailiwicks as so many personal fiefs – and to those of their subordinates who have adjusted to the rules of this game of let's-pretend, under which they take a cavalier attitude to their work without fear of losing their jobs, in exchange for their loyalty and a meagre standard of living.

But like all modernization, which undermines the traditions associated with age-old peasant culture, the process also arouses the fears of those who believe that the secularization of society poses a threat to moral or religious values, and who see unchecked industrialization as endangering the natural environment. From the ruins of official Marxism-Leninism (in which everybody has ceased to believe) a new debate is now arising, reminiscent of the nineteenth-century opposition between Slavophiles and Westernizers. Today the dividing line runs between advocates of a Marxist renewal, stressing economic reforms, and the 'idealists' hostile to foreign influences; the latter seek to uphold the 'Russian ideal' and regard themselves as the heirs to the great Russian writers and philosophers of the past. The outcome of the present confrontation therefore concerns much more than the political sphere alone, however decisive that remains: it affects the future of the nation's culture as a whole.

THE EXTENT OF THE CRISIS

The greater freedom of expression now granted to the press and writers under the rubric of glasnost allows us to form a more precise idea of the difficulties currently facing the leadership. This is not just an economic crisis, which could be tackled by means of appropriate measures: the very social fabric – the regime first and foremost – is ailing, and by extension the system as a whole.

THE ECONOMIC CRISIS
The economic crisis is felt most sharply in worsening food shortages and rising prices, which affect the great mass of the population.

The root cause of the crisis is stagnating farm output. In 1987 this grew by less than the increase in the population (respectively 0.2 per cent and 1 per cent in 1986).[1] Private stockbreeding, which was expected to give a quick boost to the production of animal products, has declined by 200,000 head of livestock in spite of incentives to families to increase their flocks under contract. This means that, instead of increasing the supply of meat and milk, 200,000 rural families are adding to the demand for these products.

How are we to account for this situation? Nothing has changed on the collective farms, in spite of promises of autonomy for the kolkhozes and sovkhozes. They remain subject to the dictates of the regional authorities, which lay down their plans of sowing and deliveries to the state in conditions that sometimes become absurd: the writer Boris Mozhayev relates that one sovkhoz was recently ordered to plant potatoes in frozen ground. 'A pyramid of desks has crushed all stirrings of initiative. The individual is accustomed to being a mere executant.'[2] Moreover, prices paid for farm produce are generally below actual costs, which will hardly induce anyone to produce more. Under these circumstances, compulsory deliveries are in fact a form of taxation in kind. 'Unpaid work in the fields and in the kolkhoz breeds a lazy, cunning [*lukavyi*] worker.'[3] This mentality explains why it is so difficult to revive the peasants' traditional spirit of enterprise – on which Gorbachev's farm policy relies. The sense of enterprise is needed to boost production, through contracts between collective farms and family plots (*semeinyi podryad*).[4]

In the private sector, the first reason for the decline is the rural exodus. Fringe rural areas in the Russian provinces outside the black-earth lands lost 5 million inhabitants between 1971 and 1986, and 725,000 *izba*s (traditional peasant homes) were abandoned.[5] Young women are the first to go, having no wish to remain dairymaids all their lives; the young men then follow, unable to find a girl to marry in the village. Efforts have been made to stem the exodus by moving the peasants to urban-style rural centres, but life in an apartment house is ill-suited to a family stockbreeding venture. Nor do the 'anti-kulak' prejudices of the local authorities encourage peasants to step up their family output. They are waiting to see which way the wind is blowing before undertaking anything.

For similar reasons, cottage industries and co-operative ventures, which were intended to make good the shortcomings of state-run production, are developing very slowly, except in the Baltic provinces: there were 14,000 co-operatives employing 150,000 people in operation at the beginning of May 1988. That is a mere drop in the bucket, given the size of the USSR. Since the promulgation of the 1986 act legalizing these activities, there has been a proliferation of private restaurants, taxis, hairdressing salons, small garment workshops, and art markets such as the one at Izmailovo near Moscow: in other words, activities that do not depend on raw materials, which are practically unobtainable other than on the open market, since the co-operatives are not entitled to the supplies available to state firms.

Supply difficulties and the lack of competition (which often put co-operatives in a monopoly position) are driving up prices without necessarily improving services to the population. Customers complain of having to pay high prices for items that are sometimes neither clean nor good.[6] For their part, the co-operatives are burdened by crushing taxation.[7] A new law on 26 May 1988 revised this unwarranted level of taxation,[8] abolished the need for prior authorization before opening a co-operative,[9] and allowed any citizen to join a co-operative (membership had previously been confined to pensioners and students). These changes are meant to enable co-operatives to hire workers laid off from the state sector.

In industry, employees have the impression that the new 1987 Law on the State Enterprise, which accorded them managerial autonomy as of 1988, is being torpedoed by the ministries. State orders (*goszakazy*), which take priority, absorb practically all of their production capacity, leaving them very little room to enter into commercial contracts.[10] Many managers claim to receive more directives than before 1988. Further, the ministries continue to skim their profits, making a mockery of the notion of the firms' financial autonomy.[11]

Among the blue-collar workers, the ones who suffer the most from this chaotic planning, there is growing resentment of 'the Gosplan and Gossnab bureaucrats, who live untouchable in their comfortable apartments, concerned only with holding on to their empires'.[12]

The deficits of the state enterprises – covered by state subsidies, without any real compensation from the market for consumer goods – fuels inflation.[13] In 1987, retail sales were up 9.2 billion rubles from the previous year, while unspent additional earnings added 24 billion rubles to savings accounts. In Moscow, an estimated 25 per cent of sums on deposit represent a form of forced savings, for want of goods to buy.[14] Specialists are hunting high and low to identify savings corresponding to illegal earnings.[15] Really smart people have several savings accounts: in 1985 one depositor in four in the USSR had two passbooks, and in the countryside, one kolkhozian in two did so.[16]

THE SOCIAL CRISIS

Rumours of a possible monetary reform to mop up surplus cash, which have generated a flight from money into valuables; fears of further price increases, coming on top of disguised increases (by taking low-priced goods off the market and replacing them with more expensive ones); the threat of layoffs (for surplus bureaucrats first of all, estimated at 18 million employees)[17] – all these factors are casting a cloud over the social climate.

The poet Yevtushenko complained recently that, seventy years after the Revolution, ration books were still in use in certain towns, and that someone had done him a favour by giving him a packet of sugar.[18] This sugar shortage hits even the big cities such as Moscow and Kiev; normal supplies of sugar have been diverted to the manufacture of moonshine liquor ever since the campaign against alcohol focused on cutting industrial production of vodka and cutting back liquor-store hours. Official liquor sales totaled 51 billion rubles in 1984, or 16 per cent of consumer spending; by 1987 the figure had fallen to 35 billion rubles. But the revenue lost to the government now lines the pockets of the bootleggers, even though those lost tax receipts – 1.5 to 2 billion rubles – could well have been used to import much-needed consumer goods.[19] In the towns, an illiterate grandmother can earn as much as a scientist by lining up to wait for the liquor store to open. In some northern regions, helicopter pilots and physicians, who are exempt from restrictions on vodka, have become highly popular overnight. Some thirsty drinkers have succumbed to the charms of alcohol-based perfumes or medications. More troubling is the use of chemical substitutes, which are inducing addiction among some young people.[20] The failure of the anti-alcohol campaign was a foregone conclusion: there was little chance of changing ingrained habits in two or three years, simply by decree.

These economic factors, some of them short-term, are merely the most visible symptoms of deeper social problems, deeply rooted in social divisions. For, far from being classless and free of conflicts, Soviet society is stratified into many different social groups, with distinctive lifestyles and levels of consumption, culture, political power, and status.

At the top of the hierarchy stand the members of the *nomenklatura* – all those who hold their jobs at the Party's discretion, whose domestic staff (secretaries, bodyguards, personal chauffeurs) enjoy the same respect as their masters.[21] Other members of the establishment include artists, writers, and people in the performing arts, who enjoy 'caste' (the word used in Russian) comparable to those of the first category, through their professional unions.[22] Far below, at the base of the pyramid, stand the mass of workers, who have trouble making ends meet because their per capita income is less than 100 rubles per month: a third of the population of the USSR falls into this category.[23] Between these two groups comes the Soviet petty bourgeoisie, which, for want of broader intellectual or spiritual horizons, finds consolation in 'the rush for objects' (*veshchizm*) – for all those baubles and gadgets, preferably labeled 'imported', that are the stuff of the Soviet consumer's dreams.

Discussion of these inequalities has been taboo until now. A recent film portraying this 'undeclared class warfare' was banned.[24] It takes its title, *Forbidden Area,* from the fact that a certain stratum of society lives in restricted neighborhoods filled with official residences and travels in black limousines, sheltered from the cares and worries of the common man, immune from criticism.[25] Official statistics are still silent about the extent of inequality, confining themselves to publishing meaningless averages.[26] For instance, the *Official Yearbook* tells us that average floorspace for each inhabitant in Soviet towns is 14.3 square metres;[27] but more detailed investigation of the distribution of housing in crowded Moscow shows 27 per cent of the population to be poorly housed (with less than 5.2 square metres per person, or living in rooms without modern conveniences).[28] Similarly, in health care, the hospitals and clinics are so overcrowded that it has proved necessary to open fee-paying clinics for Muscovites wanting more skillful treatment or more attentive care.[29]

On the fringes of Soviet society, young people form a transient social group, either because they do not yet have paid jobs or because they reject established norms. They are too diverse for us to be able to attribute a common lifestyle to them all (see chapter 3 on this point). They do, though, share a measure of nonconformism that expresses their protest at the society of their elders, which robs them of responsibility, indeed seeks to decide their future through its control of education and jobs. The youth counterculture does not deserve the name ('today's youth knows no art or literature beyond what the TV screen imposes on it'[30]) or the apprehensiveness it arouses; youth in every age has been rebellious by nature, adopting provocative fashions to demonstrate its difference from its elders. That is why youth has become something of a political battleground between those who point to rising juvenile delinquency and drug addiction to condemn the permissiveness of the authorities, and those who ascribe these evils to the corrupting influence of the West rather than regarding them as an expression of unsatisfied emotional needs. Whatever the case may be, Soviet youth may seem blasé, but it is searching for an ideal and is always the first to rally to any noble cause, be it ecological or national.

THE POLITICAL CRISIS
Against their will, young conscripts found themselves at the mercy of the war in Afghanistan, which in the eight years before May 1988 cost the USSR 13,310 killed, 311 missing, and 37,478 wounded.[31] The impact of the war was far greater than that, though, since an estimated 700,000 Soviet soldiers served in Afghanistan at some time during the intervention. This war on foreign soil was no more popular than was the Vietnam War in America, judging by the reactions of the young Latvian conscripts in Podnieks's 1986 film *Is It Easy to Be Young?*[32]

The four-party agreement of 14 April 1988, which called for the withdrawal of the Soviets' contingent of 115,000 from Afghanistan over a nine-month period starting 15 May 1988, thus resolved one of the prime causes of concern to Soviet parents.[33]

But the results of this ill-fated intervention, which was launched in December 1979 despite advice to the contrary by certain specialists,[34] have left opinion divided and uneasy. The Soviet military command, having had to swallow its first military failure, is keeping a low profile, leaving the field open to those who reject the gung-ho war literature and propaganda.[35] The writer Vyacheslav Kondratiev has seized the opportunity to remind readers of what it was really like to be a soldier in the last world war,[36] while the thoughts of Alexander Adamovich are for the 'mothers of those who did not return' from Afghanistan.[37] To be sure, it would be unrealistic to see in this the emergence of a pacifist movement in the USSR, which would no more be tolerated by those in power than are conscientious objectors. Still, for the first time the press is publishing letters from readers pondering the relationship between arms spending and Soviet living standards: 'People need to know why our standard of living is low.'[38] This in fact merely summarizes the official thesis submitted to the 28 June Party conference concerning 'the need to ensure security by political means, without allowing ourselves to be dragged further into the arms race, which could not fail to affect the level of economic and social development of our country'.[39]

On the other hand, the arms lobby also gets its due, since the thesis stresses that 'we do not deny the military danger; but the effectiveness of our defence, as regards both hardware and personnel, must henceforward depend on qualitative means'.[40]

In any case, the most painful consequences of the Afghan war – which one hopes will soon be over – are likely to be felt inside the Soviet Union itself, in the highly charged arena of the national minorities and their demands.

THE NATIONAL PROBLEM IN THE USSR

It is now admitted that disturbances in the Islamic republics of Central Asia, and perhaps even the riots in Alma-Ata, are not unconnected with a growing national awareness, stimulated by the exploits of the Afghan mujaheddin and kept alive by the clandestine activities of the Sufi communities, which are hard at work spreading Islamic fundamentalism.[41] It is well known too that at the start of the Soviet intervention in Afghanistan, the frontier troops made up of Tadzhik and Uzbek nationals had to be relieved by units drawn from other regions in order to avoid the risk of contagion.

But there are also more direct factors responsible for the resurgence of nationalism, namely the purges of the *nomenklatura* in these republics as part of the campaign against nepotism and corruption.[42] There are economic discontents as well. The administrative reform embarked on by Moscow has resulted in the abolition of some fourteen federal republic ministries, which have been replaced by departments directly under the authority of a federal ministry, thereby curbing the autonomy of the republics' administrations. Further, the central government's investment policy favours the modernization of existing industrial firms (mainly in Russia) over the creation of new ones (notably in Central Asia) – despite the availability of manpower that would justify the creation of jobs in these regions. On that point, K. Ikramov considers it an insult that Russian demographers have accused the peoples of Central Asia of traditionally having too many children.[43]

The most sensitive area of inter-ethnic relations is the linguistic issue, since it is through its national language that a people perpetuates its culture. The policy of imposing Russian as the second language is viewed with concern – especially when it goes hand in hand with the closure of national schools,[44] when university professorships in national literature are abolished, as in the Ukraine, when print runs of books in minority languages are drastically reduced,[45] or when intellectuals from the peripheral republics wishing to attend congresses abroad encounter difficulties.[46]

In addition to language, the safeguarding of natural resources and respect for the integrity of national history are favored topics for demands by the intelligentsia in the republics – as with the Ukrainians, who were awakened to the dangers of atomic energy by the Chernobyl disaster,[47] with the Estonians, who have become concerned over expanding production of phosphorites, and with the Armenians, worried about the falling level of Lake Sevan. All this has reached the point where the last writers' congress was dubbed the Ecology Congress, as practically each speaker chose to speak about some ecological theme affecting his region. The writers from Central Asia have usually been more concerned with falsifications of the history of their respective peoples[48] and the repression that they have suffered – either en masse, such as the forty thousand victims in Uzbekistan in 1940, or individually, as in the cases of certain writers unjustly accused of nationalism.[49] But more recently, the ecological disaster that destroyed the pastureland in the vicinity of the Aral Sea – turning it into either swamp or salt marshes, necessitating the uprooting of the Karakalpaks, a pastoral people that has lived on this land for centuries – underscores how important it is for some of these nationalities to protect the environment.[50]

Territorial conflicts between nationalities have dominated the news in recent months, and they are unlikely to die down soon. The demands of the Crimean Tatars (who were deported to Central Asia at the end of World War II) for the return of their autonomous republic have been rejected by the Special Commission on National Problems of the Presidium of the Supreme Soviet, on the grounds that the Crimea is now inhabited predominantly by Russians and Ukrainians; however, they are no longer prohibited from returning to settle there. This decision has not put an end to Tatar demonstrations.[51] Another Muslim nationality also deported to Central Asia, the Meskhets, traveled to Borzhomi in Georgia to demonstrate on 8 June 1988 for the right to return to that republic.

The most serious conflict is the one between the Republic of Armenia, whose population is traditionally Christian, and the predominantly Shiite Muslim Republic of Azerbaijan (adjacent to Iran), over the autonomous region of Nagorno-Karabakh, an enclave in the latter republic whose population of 175,000 is three-quarters Armenian. In May and June 1988, this population held repeated strikes in the regional capital, Stepanakert, to demand the reunification of their region with the Republic of Armenia; meanwhile, mass demonstrations have been held in Yerevan, the capital of Armenia, in support of this demand. The Azeris, meanwhile, have reacted violently, even to the point of perpetrating a pogrom in Sumgait (Azerbaijan) that is reported to have left around thirty dead and a hundred or so injured. Even though the Kremlin has responded to these disturbances by appointing new first secretaries to head the Parties of these two republics, the movements have not yet abated. The Supreme Soviet of Armenia voted on 13 June 1988 in favor of reunification, while on the same day its opposite number in Azerbaijan voted against it. *Pravda* has twice had to acknowledge the inability of the authorities to bring the situation under control,[52] and the army has had to be sent in to help prevent the exodus of the minorities concerned from one republic to the other. To break the deadlock, pending a decision by the Supreme Soviet of the USSR, the authorities in Nagorno-Karabakh have suggested that the autonomous region be directly attached to the federal echelon, and they encouraged strikers to return to work on the eve of the party conference so as not to weaken Gorbachev vis-à-vis his opponents, who might take advantage of these disturbances to attack his liberal policies.

But the deadlock is likely to persist, because the Krem-

lin cannot count on time to cool the conflict, nor can it
countenance a modification of the administrative bounda-
ries of republics without opening the door to new rectifica-
tions elsewhere.[53] Clearly it is the weakness of the central
authorities that has created the current political crisis.

THE CRISIS OF AUTHORITY

The vast range of functions that the Communist Party of
the USSR has gathered to itself has in fact resulted in a
dilution of central power, which has become so compartmentalized that it can no longer effectively govern the
whole empire it wishes to embrace. And recent stories of
corruption throughout the machine and revelations about
the history of the Party – particularly about Leonid Brezhnev's reign, some of which concern leading figures still in
office – are hardly likely to revive the Party's prestige.

Moscow has little control over what goes on in the provinces. Regional and local authorities ignore central directives whenever they think they can do so with impunity:
'Moscow,' the saying goes, 'does not rule here' (*Moskva
nam ne ukaz*).[54] The provincial press is still controlled by
the local leaders, who install 'their' men in editorial positions.[55] Journalists would be ill-advised to publish an article without first submitting it to the local official or agency
in question. This helps explain the different situations
observed in the capital and in the provinces.

'Our problem is not to eliminate the Party from public
life,' said one observer, 'but to restore to it the power that
it no longer effectively wields.'[56] Even the most radical
advocates of perestroika call for firm measures by Moscow
to reassert its authority.[57] Their advice to apply authoritarian methods to purge the Party and the administration is
tantamount to calling for the perpetuation of the Stalinist
model they want to do away with. But on the other hand,
they realize that seeking to 'transform' the nation by means
of free, democratic elections would merely give their opponents time to organize a counterattack.

What the reformers are in fact having to contend with is not so much a structured, organized opposition as a simmering resistance. It occurs at every level of the Party and government:

- In the central apparatus, Gorbachev has gradually brought supporters into the Politburo and the Secretariat. On the other hand, the Central Committee, which votes on general policy directives, remains dominated, even after the 28 June party conference, by members appointed under Brezhnev; Gorbachev does not have a safe majority in that body.
- In the administration, officials threatened by cuts in the number of ministries[58] are making common cause with company managers who fear having to shoulder the responsibilities that go with financial autonomy. 'This alliance of technocrats and bureaucrats represents a colossal pyramid which is girding itself for the counterattack.'[59] A fortiori, rural dignitaries at the local levels are still masters in their own districts.

The transition from taking orders to a culture of responsibility, in which efficiency and rigor become the rule for all, is not an easy one. It takes not only time but perseverance as well. For the fact is that the system which it is proposed to rebuild was perfectly comfortable and has more supporters at the grass roots than at the apex of the hierarchy. The leadership appears to be paralyzed, or at least ill at ease; there is a sense of indecision even at the top (*sumyatitsa*).

THE CONTENDING IDEOLOGICAL CURRENTS

If one decides to abandon coercion, as Mikhail Gorbachev apparently has, then one has no option but to rely on widely shared values. To articulate and mobilize those

values, and to overcome the resistance of those who cling
to the past, Gorbachev has turned to social groups that
have played no part in political life until now, and which
therefore enjoy a measure of moral credibility among the
population.

THE WORLD OF LETTERS

Even when courted by those in power, the intelligentsia
have always held aloof.[60] In Khrushchev's day, they used
to poke fun at his boorish ways. The literary thaw in the
1960s brought an opening onto the intimate sphere and
themes of personal experience, but it rarely (except in the
case of Dudintsev, Oveshkin, and Zhaskin) ventured into
the field of social criticism. Glasnost has restored the traditional, pre-Revolutionary, function of the writer in Russia,
which is to speak for and mold public opinion. The writer
is 'committed' to public life whether he likes it or not; the
essay on social problems (*publitsistika*) has become the
principal literary genre.

To those who wonder whether there is such a thing as
public opinion in the Soviet Union, committed writers
point to the success of the ecological campaigns. Some of
these have mobilized public opinion and forced the authorities to back down on major projects, such as the plan to
divert the rivers of Siberia and the Far North toward the
southern lands.[61] But these victories are never final when
one is dealing with administrations that feel bound to justify their existence by means of ambitious projects – and
have the money to do it.[62]

Glasnost has yet to produce a great work. Today's tal-
ented youngsters are finding it difficult to get into print
because their elders, who hold all the key jobs, are giving
priority to the great works of past decades that had hitherto
been banned – Pasternak's *Dr. Zhivago; We,* by Zamyatin;
Chevengur, by Platonov – or to contemporary works that
had until recently been hidden in the bottom drawer for the
same reason – Rybakov's *Children of the Arbat; Pushkin*

House, by Bytov; *Zhizn i Sud'ba*, by Vassily Grossman. These are the writings of a generation that had experienced many ordeals – sometimes civil war, and in practically all cases the 1930s and the Second World War. The period they deal with was an unpleasant one, and until now it was considered good manners to forget about it.

But prose writers are not alone in finding an audience: poets still stand highest in the public's esteem, and now readers are able to read poems never before published in the USSR, by Akhmatova, Tsvetayeva, Kluyev, Tvardovsky, Shalamov, and even the Nobel Prize–winning poet Leon Brodsky, who has emigrated to the United States.

It is hard to say where this 'liberalization' is going to stop: will it one day be possible to publish the early-twentieth-century Russian spiritualist philosophers (Soloviev, Berdyaev, Florovsky),[63] and recently emigrated authors (Solzhenitsyn, Sinyavsky, Voinovich, etc.)? Today, that depends as much on official directives (*Glavlit*) as on the decisions of the directors of the literary reviews.

Through these literary reviews there is now emerging a panorama of divergent tendencies and a debate about ideas – never totally free of politics – that is giving the cultural life of the nation a vitality not seen for decades. As pointed out earlier, we are witnessing a resurgence of the old divisions between Slavophiles (nowadays known as 'Russianists') and the 'Westernizers' (or, earlier, the *vekhovtsy*, or 'idealists', and the 'liberal Marxists'), who are once more asking, 'Where are we going?'

Two particular points emerge in this discussion: What is one to make of Stalin? What should be the role of spiritual values in the moral regeneration of society?

STALIN AND THE BLANK PAGES
IN THE HISTORY BOOKS

Although history is becoming a topic for debate, the historians are not taking part – they are adopting a prudent silence as long as they cannot consult the most important records. Essential documents such as those of the Politburo, which are part of the Party archives, or those of the General Staff, which are part of the Defense Ministry archives, are no more accessible than are those of the KGB, the MVD (Interior Ministry), or the MID (Ministry of Foreign Affairs).[64] The leading figures in the historical sciences under Brezhnev still run the historical institutes and reviews.[65]

The opening shots in the historical debate on Stalin were fired by a series of memoirs and works of the imagination by writers who, in portraying the past, were concerned primarily with the present – seeking to exorcise the Stalinist model, which is still very present in Soviet institutional practice and popular attitudes.

To break with Stalinism, the first need is to analyse its origins. Analyses based on Stalin's own neurotic personality, such as Rybakov's portrayal of an Asiatic despot, are a trifle facile. Grossman's view, which ascribes the excesses of the period to the cultural level of the masses of those times, transposing the characteristic intolerance and savagery of the peasant jacqueries to the nation as a whole, is more convincing. Roy Medvedev denounces Stalin's usurpation of power in the name of socialism under threat, in which he succeeded in imposing an iron discipline on the Party, reviving in the 1930s a 'war communism' whose legitimacy sprang from the philosophy of the citadel under siege.[66] As a Christian, meanwhile, I. Shafarevich refuses to distinguish between Stalinism and socialism: according to him, the very philosophy of socialism condemns the individual to being nothing but a cog in society.[67]

For those who fought in 1941–45, these views are intolerable – especially for professional soldiers, for whom Stalin was the man who galvanized the people and led them to victory, and who embodies the industrial and social conquests of the regime. The 'Stalin phenomenon', analysed by Dimitri Volkogonov, assistant to the general in charge of the Political Department of the army, typifies this reaction.[68] Some of Stalin's greatest admirers, such as Vadim Kozhinov, have even gone so far as to suggest that the 'personality cult' was the work of foreign intellectuals (he cites Henri Barbusse, Bernard Shaw, Romain Rolland, and Einstein); that it was the Jews, not Stalin, who were responsible for the destruction of the Old Moscow (Kaganovich); that it was Yakov (Epstein) Yakovlev who was responsible for the forced collectivization of the peasantry. One need hardly point out the antisemitism underlying this kind of argument published in the Russianists' review.[69]

Similarly, attempts to equate socialism with Stalinism are unacceptable to liberal Marxists such as Roy Medvedev and Fedor Burlatsky.[70] For the latter, 'barracks socialism' draws its inspiration more from Bakunin than from Marx. He contrasts the 'war communism' model with the New Economic Policy model, when the country's economy recovered swiftly.[71] Nowadays, the NEP serves to justify the concept of a noncoercive mixed economy – dependent on individual initiative, particularly in agriculture, and on allowing co-operative forms to develop spontaneously without stifling the peasant family economy – and a freer society combined with pluralism inside the Party. That is the reason for rehabilitating past victims of dogmatism (such eminent scientists as Vavilov, Kondratiev, and Chayanov), and of the great show trials of 1936–38 (Bukharin, Rykov, and Rakovsky in 1987, and Kamenev, Zinoviev, Radek, and Pyatakov on 13 June 1988 – all except Trotsky). For these liberal Marxists, the solution lies not in dismantling the state, but in allowing civil society to play its part. But on what basis?

'NATIONAL' VALUES OR 'UNIVERSAL' VALUES?
The opposition between the traditionalists and the neo-Marxists is especially evident in the sphere of values. On

the one side are the Russianists, who extol the ancient
virtues of the peasant community and call for a return to
Christian morality (the image of Christ has reappeared in
contemporary literature, notably with Aitmatov and Tendryakov[72]); opposing them are the 'realists'. While the
latter acknowledge the need to make allowance for man's
spiritual needs, they reject the identification of morality
with tradition, preferring to speak of 'universal human
values', hoping to avoid the revival of notions of a 'Russian
ideal' liable to fuel the people's latent chauvinism and
antisemitism.

'Russianists' such as Vassily Belov, Victor Astafiev, and
Valentin Rasputin have been attacked for extolling the
obshchina (the traditional peasant community, which, crit-
ics argue, was merely a 'form of slavery'), and for wanting
to keep individuals under discipline rather than setting
man free.[73] Rasputin replies that 'the old ideals may be
faded, but they were ideals, whereas perestroika is concerned primarily with the means of existence,'[74] and Astafiev takes up the theme: 'The people are tired. . . . What
they want are goodness, compassion. We have forgotten
those simple human words such as soul, love for one's
neighbour. All we ever hear about nowadays is fight, struggle; the struggle for the harvest, the struggle for cement.
We must associate this fight with the soul. That is what the
Church Fathers grasped, even though for many years we
have dismissed religion as obscurantism.'[75] It is not easy
to establish a dialogue between those whose priority is the
quest for an ideal or who call upon the conscience of the
individual,[76] and those who argue in terms of political
alternatives and the struggle to be waged.

The arch-adversary is Pamyat ('memory'), an association
that originally consisted of Russians intent on preserving
their cultural heritage. But since the official Foundation for
Culture was formed to serve that purpose, Pamyat has
gradually turned into an ultranationalist political rallying
point.[77] It enjoys the support of certain Russian writers,[78]

and very likely also has supporters inside the central Party machine and the General Staff.[79]

In the days of Tsar Nicholas I, the motto of the tsarist regime was a trinity: 'autocracy, nationalism, orthodoxy'. What is the condition of that trinity now?

The totalitarianism of the official Marxist-Leninist ideology far outdoes the autocracy of the old regime, thanks to the modern instruments available to today's regime.

Nationalism is on the brink of replacing Soviet communism as the overriding value. This is a reaction observed in all crisis-ridden societies.[80]

Will the redefinition of the relationship between church and state now in progress restore the Orthodox Church to an official place in the system?

THE ORTHODOX CHURCH

The celebrations marking the thousandth anniversary of the conversion of Rus to Christianity provided an occasion to announce new legislation to improve the status of the Orthodox Church and, collaterally, that of other religions.

The Council of the Orthodox Church that met at the Monastery of the Trinity and Saint Sergei at Zagorsk, 6–9 June 1988, stole a march on this legislation. It restored the internal status of the parishes (which had been modified by the state in 1961), placing responsibility for running the parish in the hands of the priest, rather than in those of a lay member of the parish council, appointed by the local authorities.

The new legislation is expected to confer legal status upon the churches, allowing them to own property and to defend their rights in the courts.[81] More resources will be made available for religious publications. Religious education remains prohibited, however, outside the privacy of the family.

The church has lost no time recovering its property: the

oldest monastery in the country, the eleventh-century structure known as the Grottoes, was partially handed back to the monks on 7 June 1988, while the St. Daniil Monastery in Moscow has been returned to the bishops. On the occasion of the thousandth anniversary, the state authorized the publication of 100,000 copies of the Bible and imported another 150,000, making almost as many for 1988 alone as the 350,000 copies printed in the USSR since 1917.

Believers have until now been barred from carrying out social work. This too has now been authorized, albeit within limited spheres such as assistance to hospital patients, to pensioners in homes for the elderly, or to the mentally handicapped – in other words, in areas notoriously short of personnel (in Moscow alone, there are twenty thousand vacancies for nurses).[82]

This new attitude on the part of the authorities is, in the first place, an acknowledgement that the official atheism has made little impact on a people that has clung to its beliefs. As Konstantin Kharchev, chairman of the Council for Religious Affairs attached to the government of the USSR (more or less equivalent to a Minister for Religious Affairs), said: 'One cannot abolish belief by administrative means, for the religious conception of the world will persist. Between 1971 and 1988, 30 million children were baptized into the Orthodox Church in the USSR. Further, the April 1985 directives of the plenum of the Party Central Committee stressed the need to abolish hindrances to the exercise of freedom of conscience for all citizens. At a time when our government is establishing its relations with the United States on the basis of reciprocal confidence, why should we distrust our own citizens? We ought to allow believers to feel secure as full-fledged citizens.'[83] Gorbachev, receiving the Patriarch Pimen at the Kremlin on 29 April 1988 (the last comparable meeting took place between the Patriarch and Stalin, in 1943), gave official blessing to this desire to set relations between church and state on a new footing.

The solemn celebration of the thousandth anniversary in Moscow, Zagorsk, and Kiev took place in the presence of dignitaries from a hundred countries (including the Archbishop of Canterbury, Robert Runcie; the chief rabbi of New York, Arthur Schneider; the American evangelist Billy Graham; and nine Roman Catholic cardinals), and some of the ceremonies were broadcast on Soviet TV. The favourable impact on international opinion was a boon to the authorities. Beyond such benefits, though, lie considerations of domestic politics, with the hope of mobilizing Christians in the drive to restore morality and so contribute to the orderly functioning of society.[84] The Orthodox Church 'extols love and mercy, denounces idleness and money-grubbing, and inculcates in people moral standards that are needed in our socialist society.'[85]

The official attitude is ambiguous – for, not content with seeking to secure a docile instrument by retaining control over clerical appointments, those in power are aiming at a farther-reaching alliance. In a confidential report to the Council on Religious Affairs, Kharchev has written: 'Our history has shown that religion is with us for good and all. It is easier for the Party to turn a sincere believer into someone who believes in communism also. We are now encountering the following problem: we need to educate a new type of priest; that is the job of the Party . . . . The activities of the Russian Orthodox Church are controlled, and these limited initiatives are no cause for concern, although neither is the patience of a whipped dog without limit. What worries us is the growing strength of the other faiths: the Catholic Church, which keeps on popping up,[86] and the other sects, which continue to flourish.'[87]

The present modus vivendi with the Russian Orthodox Church cannot satisfy believers, who reject state interference in church affairs and the limitations placed on it –

notably in regard to religious education.[88] Nor does it satisfy those who, without belonging to the church, demand a clear separation between church and state rather than a privileged status for it, on the grounds that the confusion between ideology and religion is prejudicial to both.[89] Nor, of course, can it satisfy Party militants, raised as atheists. The latter want at all costs to avoid anything likely to aid and abet the nationalist current, for a national-religious ideology could become a serious rival to the Party. Hence the cautious tone of certain official statements, confining themselves to acknowledging the 'impact of Christianization on Medieval Russian culture and history, without going so far as to claim that Christianity was the basis of this culture, and without joining in the celebrations of the thousandth anniversary of the church.'[90]

THE POLITICAL STRUGGLE

'Two years of waffling have merely aggravated social inequalities and lowered real incomes for the majority of the population. Food shortages, the prevailing laxity toward youth, the freedom to engage in religious propaganda, the decentralization of culture, the freedom to emigrate, public discussion of sexual problems and those dealt with by the social sciences which are deleterious to moral health, the abolition of compulsory military service, the introduction of pluralism: all these ideas come from the enemies of socialism.' Those barbed terms appeared in a letter from a reader, Nina Andreyeva, to *Sovetskaya Rossiya* on 13 March 1988, attacking the present reforms. After reminding readers of the high growth rates achieved by the centralized system in the early five-year plans, the article went on to propose the 'establishment of a strong state, capable of mobilizing society for the achievement of grandiose social programs'.

Three weeks passed before *Pravda* riposted, on 5 April

1988, with an attack on what it claimed was the manifesto of the conservatives. That a simple letter from a reader should have provoked an editorial in *Pravda* was evidence that the letter had in fact been inspired by the entourage of Yegor Ligachev, who is regarded as the leader of the opposition to Gorbachev's initiatives.[91] Hostilities between the two were thus brought into the open.

The first signs of differences of outlook between the two men became apparent in the summer of 1987, when Ligachev was acting Party chief while Gorbachev was on vacation.[92] It looks as if these differences concern less the need for perestroika than the manner and pace of reform. Gorbachev is thought to favor a faster pace, Ligachev a more measured appraisal of the past. During the November 1987 celebrations of the seventieth anniversary of the Revolution, Gorbachev was unable to avoid giving his own measured, though positive, assessment of Stalinism. At the Central Committee plenum on 21 October 1987, the ebullient Boris Yeltsin, whom Gorbachev had placed at the head of the Moscow Gorkom in order to carry out an exemplary purge,[93] was accused of 'adventurism'. He was forced to resign on 13 November 1987. The conservative clan had scored a victory.

At the approach to the selection of delegates to the Party conference called to approve a new phase in the process of restructuring, the reformers were under pressure to retaliate. The *Pravda* editorial of 5 April 1988 came to stand as a countermanifesto on 'the principles of reorganization: a revolutionary way of thought and action', denouncing the 'profoundly conservative and dogmatic position' of the *Sovetskaya Rossiya* article. Opponents of reform want to 'perpetuate an order in which bureaucracy, corruption, bribery, and petty-bourgeois degeneracy are rife . . . . By defending Stalin, some people have sought to preserve in our lives today, in our practice, the right to arbitrary decisions and the norms that he implanted in the Party and in society. Worse still, they uphold the right to arbitrary decision-making and self-interest in the guise of personal infallibility.'

The counteroffensive continued with a series of meetings between Gorbachev and the party leaders of the different republics (11, 14, and 18 April 1988), and with representatives of the media (7 May) in order to prepare for the Central Committee meeting of 23 May, which was intended to approve the Politburo's 'theses' for the conference on 28 June.

As was to be expected, the theses published in *Pravda* on 27 May 1988 represent a compromise – in style, and still more in substance. While reformists could claim that it opened the way to substantive change, conservatives noted with satisfaction that the Party remains the unchanging bedrock of the political system, 'the vanguard of the working class and of all workers. Drawing its strength from Marxist-Leninist doctrine, it is the Party's task to frame the theory and strategy of political change, to formulate the ideology of socialist renewal, to lead the political task of mass organization, to educate and assign cadres.' The Party remains the political core of each group in society. The document reaffirms the principles of democratic centralism.

Although the foundations of the system are upheld, new directions are suggested in the economic sphere. These involve ratifying reforms in progress (such as the modernization of industry, financial autonomy for companies, production contracts in farming – although family contracts, whose effectiveness Gorbachev praised at the congress of kolkhozians in March 1988, are not mentioned directly), and they pave the way for price reform – even though a cut in living standards is ruled out.

But the document is most concerned with the political sphere. Here, the planned innovations will involve the following:

- The Party's responsibilities will be more strictly delimited, since past stagnation is ascribed to the fact that the Party had taken the place of the state. On the other hand, the role of the elective state bodies – the soviets at the different levels – are expected to play a greater role and assert their preeminence over the executive organs.
- Rules of eligibility for Party office or membership in the soviets have been amended so as to avoid another gerontocracy. Five-year mandates are to be renewable once or, exceptionally, twice if approved by a three-fourths majority. To make these elections democratic, more than one candidate may run for office, and voting will be by secret ballot.
- Last but not least, it is planned to base state practice on the rule of law by means of judicial reform. Accused persons shall be deemed innocent until proved otherwise, and civil associations will be permitted, provided their activities are nor detrimental to the developmental interests of socialist soviet society. Since the state is governed by the rule of law, state officials and even Party leaders are subject to the law and may act solely within the strict bounds of the law.

To people who were hoping for more liberalization, the theses look rather tame. We shall have to await publication of the bills spelling out their precise content, but it is not too early to comment on a text that has been approved by the Politburo.

The Party is referred to as the 'single historically constituted Party,' which seems to suggest that historic, not ideological, causes account for the Party's monopoly. It still plays a part in the nomination of candidates for elections and in the selection of key cadres, which implies the maintenance of the *nomenklatura.* [94] It is pointed out that Party life will be democratized *gradually,* and that the

burgeoning plurality of opinions presupposes a whole revolutionary process in people's consciousness and a process
of ideological renewal. For the immediate future, the first
step forward will be confined to permitting open discussions and contending platforms, but within the framework
of respect for Party discipline.[95] 'They must not lead to
political confrontation, to the division of social forces,
which would complicate [efforts to] resolve problems.'[96]

The theses are silent on the subject of the problem of
resurgent nationalism – why they are must remain a matter
of political speculation – but the Party conference confirmed the Kremlin's determination not to countenance any
redrawing of frontiers. The theses confine themselves to
making provision for the decentralization of a wide range
of administrative functions within the terms of the Constitution (with the possibility of later revising the decentralization). But what Estonia and Lithuania asked their
delegates to call for at the Party conference went well
beyond administrative autonomy: what they want is con-
federate-republic status, which would make them virtually
independent in economics, finance, and customs. To protect themselves from Russification, they want the right to
take demographic measures to protect their nationality.
The Latvians' concerns are similar; they fear that they are
on their way to becoming a minority in their own republic.[97]

Informal associations will be permitted only if they acknowledge the socialist system. There is no question of
creating a party of opposition in the form attempted by the
Democratic Union. The representatives of various groups
meeting for this purpose in Moscow on 9 May 1988 were
dispersed by the police, and their leader, Sergei Grigoryants, editor of the newspaper *Glasnost*, was held for several
days and his archives were destroyed.[98] At best people will
be allowed to organize patriotic fronts in support of Party
policy, comparable to those already in existence in Poland

and Hungary.[99] These limitations, coupled with the refusal to authorize independent co-operative publishing houses, casts a pall of doubt over the prospects of the reemergence of a genuine civil society in the USSR. How can one speak of pluralism when all associations are supposed to be under Party control?

In the economic sphere, the knottiest question remaining to be solved is how to implement the price reform, which will not occur until 1991 and which 'will be spread over a fairly long period.'[100] To cushion the impact of price rises on spending power after subsidies have been abolished, officials are examining an equalizing formula to off-set increased food prices by lowering the prices of manufactured goods. But some people argue against raising farm prices, on the grounds that this would amount to perpetuating a system of high production costs resulting from inefficiency on the farm.[101] Moreover, we still know nothing about the future status of Gosplan. We do know that Ligachev favors a limited version of economic centralism. On the table now are organizational proposals inspired by the present East German model and similar to the organization of industries into a series of 'syndicates' as in the USSR at the time of the NEP.[102] Another problem about which the theses are silent is the extent to which the Soviet economy ought to be opened up to foreign trade. Nikolai Shmelev recommends that the country should resort to massive imports of consumer goods, financed by foreign borrowing, in order to alleviate current shortages as quickly as possible. Prime Minister Ryzhkov, on the other hand, is reluctant to adopt a course that has led countries such as Hungary, Poland, and Yugoslavia heavily into debt and that could impair the economic independence of the Soviet Union.

The institution of a state based on the rule of law entails a number of preconditions which Soviet jurists define as follows:[103]

- A tribunal or court of law should be set up to assess the constitutionality of laws and statutory instruments. Some jurists even call for counterweights to arbitrary power.[104] Justice ought to be immune from intervention by the authorities, here referred to as 'telephone law', whereby a Party official can call an examining magistrate.
- Citizens should be able to appeal to the tribunals from illegal decisions by the authorities. Yet the 1988 act that provides for these appeals authorizes them against individuals only and rejects them when the contested decision was made by a commission, as is the case for most administrative acts affecting everyday life (housing allocations, pensions, etc.).

To this catalogue Andrei Sakharov adds the need to bring Soviet legislation into line with international commitments entered into by the Soviet Union (Helsinki agreements) and the release of political prisoners.[105] By allowing Soviet citizens to go abroad to the country of their choice (whether on travel or to emigrate), the Kremlin would settle the tragic problem of the refuseniks, which has bedeviled its dealings with the West, at one swoop.[106] Sakharov goes on to argue that the activities of the KGB ought to be brought under judicial control, and he calls for an inquiry into complicity between the KGB and international terrorist organizations and its role in the repression of dissidents.[107]

Respect for legality for the benefit of all, including by Party organs, the preeminence of the law over the political sphere, and legal guarantees that human rights will be respected: these are the conditions upon which the Soviet people will stand behind perestroika. As long as these guarantees are not given practical effect, the population will stand passively by as the campaign unfolds, for it has seen many others in the past without becoming actively involved.

THE NINETEENTH PARTY CONFERENCE (28 JUNE TO 1 JULY 1988)

The nomination process to pick the five thousand delegates to this conference – the first since 1941 – did not give Mikhail Gorbachev the numerical backing he had been looking for. Well-known advocates of reform – such as Tatyana Zaslavskaya, president of the Association of Sociologists; economists Nikolai Shmelev and Gavril Popov (notwithstanding protests by Moscow University students); playwright Mikhail Shatrov, author of a successful play featuring Lenin and Stalin; and the dramatist A. Gullman – failed to secure election. Lacking a safe majority at the outset, Gorbachev was obliged to present a report that took account of the misgivings of the 'gradualists' (conservatives). The report was approved by the entire Politburo in the eight days prior to the opening of the conference.

The report surprised observers by the combative tone and self-assurance of Secretary Gorbachev, and by the boldness of some of its proposals, never before formulated. But Gorbachev also displayed political skill in skating round obstacles and appeasing potential opponents. The core of the report tackles the reform of the political system, subordinating improvements in the economic situation (on which he was able to present only mixed results), to an overhaul of institutions. This is rather a tall order, for never in history have we seen men in power willingly relinquishing it or allowing their privileges to be curbed.

The novel aspect was that political reform was to be based on a parliamentary system. A People's Congress of 2,250 deputies, made up of 1,500 district deputies elected for five years on a national basis, and 750 deputies appointed by the Party, the labour unions, artists' unions, and association. This People's Congress would elect the president of the Supreme Soviet by secret ballot, who would become head of state. More than one candidate would be allowed to run, and elections would be by secret ballot. The Congress would meet once a year to approve constitutional, political, social, and economic reforms; also, in addition to electing the president, it would elect the Supreme Soviet of the USSR, which would be a permanent body of 400 to 450 members.

The president would be in charge of foreign policy and defense. He would appoint the prime minister. The future head of state – who, it is unanimously agreed, would be Mikhail Gorbachev – would enjoy greater security of tenure (elected for a five-year term, renewable once) to carry out reforms, since he would derive his powers from the nation's vote; he would no longer be in danger of losing it by accident, as could happen to the Party general secretary should he be outvoted at a plenum of the Central Committee. In other words, this reform is crucial to him since it would allow him to circumvent the Politburo, not all of whose members are ardent supporters of his policies.

The majority of the delegates to the Party Conference were conservative-minded, and Gorbachev's main achievement was to reassure them as to their future. He stated from the outset that there would be no revision of the Central Committee or the governing organs during the conference; that there would be no compulsory retirement age for people in top positions, and that elected first secretaries would automatically be appointed to head the different soviets that were to be established.

Not all delegates reacted favourably to these concessions. The economist Abalkin expressed surprise that the first secretaries were to be given executive functions, even though the theses had stipulated that the Party was to have a role of political guidance, which would be separate from purely governmental activity. Gorbachev justified the apparent paradox by pointing out that his intention was not to eliminate the Party from day-to-day government but, on the contrary, to reinvigorate the political regime by subjecting it to control by popular vote, since the future first secretary would have to gain election as a deputy to the Soviet. Consequently, power would remain in the hands of a single Party, but it would have to modify its methods and discard its authoritarian style, in order to be more responsive to the needs of the population. Other delegates were surprised to see people such as Andrei Gromyko and Mikhail Solomentsev,[108] representing the now-discredited Stalinist and Brezhnev past, still in top positions. Yegor Ligachev took their defense, pointing out that they, like himself, had helped appoint the present general secretary.

While Gorbachev would have liked a broad debate on the reform of the political system, workers' delegates and factory managers spoke of highly practical problems such as shortages and the parasitic behaviour of ministerial bureaucrats. The general secretary acknowledged that the economic reform was proceeding very slowly and attributed this to the weakness of the state; in his view, this meant that priority should be given to setting up effective political mechanisms. But he also made a point of stressing, in his closing speech to the conference, that the problem of improving food supplies should be treated as a prime concern. He also emphasized the need to improve rural amenities and the status of women.[109] He said that peasants should be allowed to rent kolkhoz acreage so that they might once more feel themselves to be 'masters of their own land'. In his inaugural address, he also put in a word for believers, denouncing past administrative measures against them and calling upon communists 'not to show disrespect for the beliefs of churchgoers.'

The sharpest debate of the conference – and this was a novelty, for in more than sixty years, the Party had not witnessed comparable exchanges between its dignitaries – came in a clash between two personalities representing opposing extremes in the Central Committee. Boris Yeltsin, who had been dismissed from the Politburo for 'adventurism' in November 1987, publicly appealed for his reinstatement, while Yegor Ligachev, who is regarded as the leader of the 'temporizers', rejected the appeal.[110] Gorbachev upheld the rejection in his closing speech.

To sum up this historic conference:

- Although they met with some criticism,[111] glasnost and pluralism inside the Party came through the test with success, and they set a new style in political debate, with TV viewers witnessing certain passages. In place of the customary unanimous affirmative vote, the proposed thesis on the possibility of a third term of office and a resolution on youth were actually voted. down; also, certain amendments failed to receive the assembly's assent.[112]

- On the other hand, Gorbachev won the votes on six resolutions concerning new political institutions[113] and laying down the timetable for their implementation, namely November 1988 for the vote by the existing Supreme Soviet on the constitutional amendments; winter 1989 for the election of the new Parliament, which will meet in April 1989; fall 1989 for the new elections to the local soviets.

- Meanwhile, little has filtered through concerning the reform of the Party, other than that local elections will be held to renew the local leaderships by the end of 1988, and that Party departments duplicating state administrations will be abolished. The review of the new Party statutes has been postponed until the twenty-eighth congress, due to be held in early 1991.

At the close of the conference, Gorbachev announced unexpectedly that a monument would be erected in Moscow 'to commemorate the victims of repression'; he did not add: by Stalin. He thus satisfied Andrei Sakharov, spokesman for the movement for the memorial, and avoided offending devotees of the 'personality cult'.

Events in the summer of 1988 have induced Gorbachev to speed up the intended timetable. Either maneuvering by opponents has necessitated an immediate response, or, after a visit to Siberia where the difficulties of everyday life are most in evidence, he has grasped the depth of popular discontents and the need to strengthen the authority of the center. For this purpose, an unscheduled meeting of the Central Committee was called on 30 September 1988 to ratify the reorganization of the Central Committee Secretariat, appointing new men to head the secretariat's six commissions and shifting the balance in Gorbachev's favour. Andrei Gromyko resigned from the presidency of the Supreme Soviet, which was convened in extraordinary session the next day to elect Gorbachev to succeed him.

The departure of Gromyko, Mikhail Solomentsev, Pyotr Demichev, and Vladimir Dolgikh from the Politburo, the replacement of Yegor Ligachev as chief ideologist by Vadim Medvedev (hitherto not a member of the Politburo), and the replacement of Viktor Chebrikov as the head of the KGB by General Vladimir Kryuchkov (who has not been appointed to the Politburo) all reinforce Gorbachev's position. But that still does nothing to solve the major problems outstanding. Ligachev, now in charge of agricultural policy, is an opponent of privatization of the economy, whereas Gorbachev, by authorizing peasants in July 1988 to lease land for terms of twenty, thirty, or even fifty years, has paved the way for decollectivization. For the time being, hopes of improving food supplies are slender, that the government has had to ease up on its tough laws on the sale of alcohol. Further, national demands continue to dominate the headlines – in Armenia, where the agitation has not abated, and in the Baltic lands, especially Estonia, where the Popular Front has won the right to put up candidates at the next elections. In sum, tension still reigns in the country.

THE MORNING AFTER

Is Gorbachev's personal victory secure? Doubtless from his viewpoint, as he has said, perestroika is now irreversible, in the sense that he no longer fears open opposition to it. To achieve that, he had to present himself as a moderate centrist ready to revise his position and even acknowledge past errors of judgement. He has thus broken with traditional infallibility of his predecessors, the interpreters of the laws of history – and that could one day render him vulnerable. For in practice, his pragmatic policies are taking him into terra incognita, and the resulting hesitancy and uncertainty throughout the administration may ultimately generate new forms of inertia and possibly even a return to the habits of the past, should it prove necessary to postpone certain projects.

So nothing is truly irreversible until there has been a change in people's mentalities. That often takes more than a single generation. One of the habits Gorbachev mentions in his report is the Soviets' deepseated notion that it is contrary to socialism for someone to earn more than others by working harder or better. The sense of 'leveling' *(uravnilovka),* as the Russians call it, holds that if that one gets something, then it is only fair for everyone else to get it also. This of course runs counter to the spirit of the economic reform, which is intended to stimulate efficiency and quality in work through pay differentials. Shmelev notes that it is envy that breeds the bureaucratic mentality.[114]

Another feature of the popular mentality – for a people that has never known anything other than the 'Father of the People' (be he tsar or Stalin) and never the state based on the rule of law – is its belief that if the authorities grant one something, then one ought to be grateful to them.[115] This lackey *(lakeistvo)* mentality in dealings with authority is ill-suited to present needs, which call for managers capable of taking initiatives.[116] Servility is a failing not only of the general mass of people but of the intelligentsia as well, which too often turns to the sovereign to settle its own internecine quarrels.

In other words, perestroika is running ahead of people's mentalities (apart from a minority who have traveled abroad and seen for themselves how far behind their country now lags). Consequently, it can only hope to be a revolution from above, and to succeed, 'we need revolutionaries resolved to overcome oppositions that have outlived their usefulness.'[117] The proclaimed democratization is therefore in fact a contradiction in terms.

The outcome of the conflict between gradualists (or conservatives) and reformists determined to press onward regardless is unlikely to be settled quickly; it will, however, determine the nature of political power the historic importance to be ascribed to the present phase. Popular wisdom teaches us that victory will go to the most obstinate – not necessarily the most idealistic – protagonist. But if for the time being obstacles (in the shape of general resistance and of anticipated poor economic results in the near future), appear to be coalescing against Gorbachev, in the longer run, on the other hand, objective and subjective factors are working to open up the Soviet Union to the outside world and in favour of gradual liberalization of Soviet society.

The stronger international co-operation ushered in by the signature of a series of agreements with the United States on 1 June 1988 is the product of more than mere short-term circumstances: it is consonant with the logic of the world we live in, where no state can halt the flow of ideas or solve its problems by isolating itself from the rest of the world.

The intelligentsia, meanwhile, which is never satisfied with the present, has been restored to its function of social criticism. It is the breeding ground of new visions of society; it is the spearhead of a process that no one can halt with impunity. For if there is one lesson that the West can learn from recent developments in Russia, it is the confirmation it brings us that no regime has the power to destroy man's most precious possession, his conscience. Stalin wanted to turn the intellectual into an engineer of the soul. He failed to give birth to *Homo sovieticus,* and it is high time we consigned that scarecrow to the attic of cold-war imagery. The voices that arose from the depths went unheeded because unheard, due to censorship, but they gave rise to a body of writing that for many years languished in people's bottom drawers and is only now emerging into broad daylight. Some of those voices still languish in the camps or are condemned to exile. But together they form a swelling chorus. Like the great Russian writers of the past, they express treasures of humanism mellowed through ordeal; they express those values that – far more than the material wellbeing of which the West is so proud – can give us our true reasons for living.

Saanen, October 1988

Notes

ABBREVIATIONS

Lit. Gaz. = *Literaturnaya Gazeta*
Nash Sov. = *Nash Sovremennik*
Soc. issl. = *Sociologicheskie issledovaniya*

CHAPTER 1: NEW TRENDS IN SOVIET SOCIETY

1. For instance, the authorities in Kazakhstan dragged their feet for six months over a decision about a form of work organization condemned sixteen years ago, but now back in favor (*Lit. Gaz.*, 1 Apr. and 7 Oct. 1987).
2. 'By communism, we mean a world of exemplary well-being that not so long ago would have forced us to disbelieve what we were able to see with our own eyes' (*Soc. issl.*, no. 3, 1985, p. 109).
3. The rural population accounted for two-thirds of the total population of the Soviet Union in 1940; today it is only one-third.
4. *Soc. issl.*, no. 3, 1985, p. 109.
5. Husbands enjoy an average of ten hours more leisure time per week than their wives; often this time is spent in drinking, which is to blame for 20 per cent of divorces.
6. 'Whole regions [in Uzbekistan] have graduated from feudalism to socialism,' but the feudal mentality survives (I. Kramov, *Lit. Gaz.*, 10 June 1987); the same goes for Tadzhikistan (*Lit. Gaz.*, 12 Nov. 1986).

7. The USSR is host to an average of 3.8 million tourists and 30,000 foreign students a year. In the 1970s, when they were not jammed, the foreign radio stations (Voice of America, BBC, and Deutsche Welle) had an estimated audience of 60 million. Since May 1987, the BBC and the Voice of America have become audible once more.

8. Comprising 16.3 million people at the time of the 1979 census, among them a great many Jews, only 4 per cent of whom continue to speak their original language.

9. The non-Russian nationalities accounted for 61.3 million people at the time of the 1987 census, of whom 60 per cent were bilingual, representing an increase of 46 per cent in nine years.

10. Islam is a criterion of identification for 60 per cent of the population of Central Asia; Georgians and Armenians too retain a strong attachment to the rites of their church.

11. There is no Communist Party, army, or banking system specific to each republic. What is more, the Council of Ministers of the USSR, together with the federal ministries, is empowered to quash all decisions made within the republics.

12. Materials in 'short supply' are stolen in the enterprises; tractors and cars are dismantled during transport via railroad due to lack of surveillance (*Izvestia,* 10 Sept. 1986) to supply the illicit trade in spare parts. Coal losses are estimated at 3–5 million metric tons per year (*Nash. Sov.,* no. 4, 1987, p. 180).

13. The scale of wealth as ascertainable from a survey of 16-to-17-year-olds in 1987 was as follows (in descending order of income): sellers of foreign garments (*fartsovshchiki*), illicit traders, servicemen, workers in the far north, restaurateurs, car mechanics, ministers, hairdressers, managers, store sales staff, prostitutes, diplomats, taxidrivers, pilots, butchers, teachers (*Lit. Gaz.,* 2 Sept. 1987).

14. The magazine *Novy Mir* published Solzhenitsyn's early works during this period.

15. Overtime is calculated at 150 per cent of the basic rate for the first two hours, with double pay for any additional hours or holidays worked. In the old Gorky truck factory built by Ford in 1931, workers stay for no longer than two months due to dissatisfaction with pay and living conditions; this represents a turnover of 10,000 workers per year to the benefit of the newer Kamaz and Vaz factories (Velikonova, *Lit. Gaz.,* 9 July 1987).

16. At the instigation of Brezhnev's son-in-law, G. Gvishiani, the Institute for the Management of the National Economy, founded

in 1970, provides an introduction to management methods for leading economic officials.

17. The Central Committee turnover rate was 60 per cent in 1961, but had fallen to 28 per cent by 1976, and to 17 per cent in 1981.

18. The May 1972 and June 1973 Moscow and Washington summit meetings with Richard Nixon, and the November 1974 meeting with Gerald Ford; the signing of a series of industrial-co-operation agreements with West Germany, France, and Japan in 1974. The 1974 agreement with the United States was prevented from being ratified by the Jackson amendment, which tied this agreement to freedom to emigrate for Soviet Jews; but in 1975 a grain agreement was signed (suspended by Jimmy Carter in January 1980 after the USSR's invasion of Afghanistan in December 1979), and was extended in 1981 by Ronald Reagan.

19. The Politburo had had to rely on the help of senior Army officers to eliminate the anti-Party group of Malenkov, Molotov, Kaganovich, and Voroshilov, and in the 14 October 1964 plot against Khrushchev.

20. Output of coal and of iron and manganese ore has ceased to increase since 1978, while oil production has flattened out since 1983 (Abel Aganbegyan, *Ekonomika*, no. 11, 1985, p. 5). Because of the slump in the birth rate, surplus manpower has fallen from 11 million workers in 1981–85 to 5 million in 1986–90.

21. The political police are believed to number some 90,000 agents (not including informants [*stukachi*]), who operate undercover and enjoy awesome privileges – even abroad, since its carefully trained agents enjoy diplomatic immunity.

22. Sharaf Rashidov, who was first secretary of the Communist Party in Uzbekistan, and Dinmukhamed Kunayev, first secretary of Kazakhstan, both members of the Politburo, were expelled from the Party for corruption (the former posthumously). V. Churbanov, former minister of the interior and son-in-law of Brezhnev, and the latter's own son, Yuri Brezhnev, vice-minister of foreign trade, were indicted later on.

23. Among the principal defendants were the first secretary of the province of Rostov, who had been at the head of a whole ring; the first secretary of the district of Krasnodar; and one Yeliseyev, the manager of a big Moscow food store, who was executed in July 1984.

24. The average for the USSR, including homemade alcohol (*samogon*); the average is half as high in Central Asia, owing to Islam's ban on alcohol.

25. V. Chikin, *Sovetskaya Rossiya*, 13 Dec. 1982.

26. In April 1985, Nikolai Ryzhkov was appointed chairman of the Council of Ministers of the USSR in place of Tikhonov. Viktor Chebrikov, head of the KGB, and Yegor Ligachev, secretary for ideology (having handed over his post for secretary for cadres to Razumovsky) joined the Politburo. In June 1987 it was the turn of Alexander Yakovlev, secretary for ideology, V. Nikonov, secretary for agriculture, and N. Slyunkov, secretary for industry, to gain promotion. Lev Zaikov succeeded Boris Yeltsin at the Moscow Gorkom on 11 November 1987, but kept his seat on the Politburo.

27. Z. Mlynar related his memories of the days when Gorbachev was his fellow student at the Moscow University Faculty of Law (*Unita*, 9 April 1985).

28. A. Gromyko, *Kommunist*, no. 5, March 1985.

29. V. Molotov was even rehabilitated before his death in 1986.

30. Village prose writers (*derevenskaya proza*) were the first to describe the true state of the rural economy, and economists such as G. Lisichkin were already stressing the virtues of a market-regulated co-operative system and socialist economy in the early 1960s (*Plan i rynok*, 1966). Among others, Lisichkin cited a letter from Lenin to G. Krzhizhanovsky: 'The really big danger with state planning is that it is liable to become bogged down in bureaucracy.'

31. In certain kolkhozes in Estonia, the livestock has been entrusted to the care of family-run farms.

32. Through the intermediary of Dusko Doder, Moscow correspondent of the *Washington Post* (3 Aug. 1983).

33. D. Kurashvili, *Sovetskoe gosudarstvo i pravo*, no. 6, 1982; *Eko*, no. 3, 1983.

CHAPTER 2: THE BROAD OUTLINES OF GORBACHEV'S POLICIES

1. The recall of Anatoly Dobrynin, the Soviet ambassador in Washington, to run the Foreign Affairs Secretariat at the Central Committee, illustrates the importance attached to this goal.

2. The Western press takes great delight in recording the subtle differences of appreciation in the statements of Gorbachev and Ligachev.

3. Yakovlev studied at Columbia University in 1959, and was then ambassador to Canada for ten years. A skilled communicator, he is credited with having invented the terms 'glasnost' and 'pere-

stroika' as well as having prime responsibility for foreign propaganda.

4. Gorbachev, speaking to media officials (*Pravda*, 17 July 1987).

5. V. Ginzburg, *Lit. Gaz.*, 19 Mar. 1986. 'My boss may call me an imbecile, but I can slip into any store through the back door, and my wife doesn't have to stand in line. During the period of stagnation, this lack of self-respect was made up for by privileges. I may be forced to stand at attention before my superiors, and people may even hit me, but it is my privilege to ride in a black car, and I can ignore traffic laws.' (*Lit. Gaz.*, 30 Sept. 1987.)

6. 'An article should be a contribution to the public cause, not a reflection of one's complexes or ambitions . . . . It is intolerable to see journalists humiliating somebody instead of criticizing him.' (Gorbachev, *Pravda*, 14 Feb. 1987.)

7. *Pravda*, 5 July 1987.

8. Gorbachev, ibid. 'We shall naturally not publish any article likely to discredit the Socialist path, the heroic history of the Soviets, our Revolution, the internationalist feelings of the Soviet peoples, and the high ideals of perestroika' (A. Belyaev, chief editor of *Sovetskaya Kultura*, 6 Sept. 1987).

9. The show takes its name from the youth section, which produces this program; it occupies the twelfth floor of the TV building.

10. V. Drozdov, *Lit. Gaz.*, 30 Sept. 1987.

11. A. Belyaev, *Sovetskaya Kultura*, 6 Sept. 1987.

12. *Ogonek* has a circulation of 1.5 million; the circulation of *Literaturnaya Gazeta*, another weekly, which tackles burning topics in a lively, discussion-provoking style, has increased from 400,000 in 1967 to 3 million in 1987. *Moskovskie Novosti* (the English-language edition is called *Moscow News*), published by the Soviet Societies for Friendship and Cultural Relations with Foreign Countries, is run by the historian Yegor Yakovlev, who is sometimes criticized by his namesake at Agitprop for the boldness of some of the articles published, such as Lenin's political testament with its harsh judgements on Stalin, or news about Soviet émigrés (the magazine published an obituary for the writer Viktor Nekrasov, who died in Paris in 1987). *Novy Mir*'s circulation has increased from 500,000 to 1,150,000, and a further increase is expected in 1988. The biggest circulations are for *Komsomol'-skaya Pravda* (which has increased from 10.7 to 17.6 million) and the magazine *Yunost'* (3.1 million), while *Pravda*'s circulation is falling (*Moscow News*, 21 Feb. 1988). There has also been a revival of interest in *Uchitel'skaya Gazeta*, the standard-bearer

for perestroika in the educational sphere, its circulation having risen from 860,000 to 1.7 million.

13. *Pravda*, 15 July 1987.

14. Khrushchev pushed through a new set of statutes in 1961 providing for a 25 per cent turnover rate for the Politburo and Central Committee every five years.

15. The republics most affected were Moldavia (Vyshka, vice-chairman of the Council of Ministers), Kirghizia (T. Usubaliev, first secretary of the Central Committee), Uzbekistan (S. Rashidov, first secretary; N. Khidaiberdyev, chairman of the Council of the Ministers, and five obkom first secretaries), and Tadzhikistan in 1986; Kazakhstan, Bashkiria, and Armenia in 1987.

16. *Izvestia*, 21 Aug. 1986; a vice-minister of foreign trade, V. Suchkov, was sentenced to thirteen years' imprisonment in June 1987.

17. 'The lying figure', *Novy Mir*, no. 2, 1987, p. 181. According to this article, tonnages transported by automobile are overestimated by 20–30 per cent, the overall index of industrial output is overestimated by adding new products which are more expensive at current prices to figures expressed at constant prices in principle. This practice has not escaped the notice of the Harvard economist Alexander Gershenkron (*A Dollar Index of Soviet Machinery Output*, Rand Corporation, 1951).

18. N. Shmelev, *Novy Mir*, no. 6, 1987, p. 158.

19. J. Rosenbaum, *Lit. Gaz.*, 12 Nov. 1986.

20. If several candidates obtain more than half the votes cast, the additional candidates form a reserve pool who sit on the soviet with a consultative vote. Out of the 120,000 deputies elected in multiple-candidate constituencies, 25,000 thus form the 'reserve pool', while 1,076 candidates failed to obtain a majority.

21. *Lit. Gaz.*, 1 July 1987. More than a quarter of the eight hundred Moscow deputies belong to the leadership (*rukovoditeli*).

22. J. Rosenbaum, *Lit. Gaz.*, 12 Nov. 1986. 'Perestroika depends on substituting "professionals" for the "activists" ' (O. Popkov, *Lit. Gaz.*, 4 Mar. 1987).

23. The regions are North and West, South, Urals, and Siberia.

24. Gorbachev at the 26 June 1986 plenum.

25. Statutes on the mechanical engineering industries (August 1985); on economic development for the period of the twelfth five-year plan 1986–1990 and broad outlines until the year 2000 (twenty-seventh congress, March 1986); on the organization of foreign trade (September 1986); on enterprises (26 June 1987).

26. Abel Aganbegyan, 'Avenues to change', *Lit. Gaz.*, 18 Feb. 1987; 'Perestroika', *Ekonomika*, 1987.

27. In the space of fifteen years, growth fell from 41 per cent in the course of the eighth five-year plan to 16 per cent in the course of the eleventh five-year plan (1980–85).

28. In 1986, this branch enjoyed a 30 per cent increase over the previous year.

29. Land rents, mineral tax on raw materials, water rates.

30. The channeling of profits earned by enterprises to the ministries had been responsible for the failure of the 1965 reform, placing efficient factories on an equal footing with the laggards.

31. Twenty ministries and seventy major enterprises are no longer obliged to work through the Foreign Trade Ministry. Further, it is now possible to form joint-venture (*sovmestnoe predpriatie*) enterprises with foreign firms. Some have already been formed with Finland. It is also planned to make the ruble convertible, but convertibility with the West is unlikely in the immediate future (A. Aganbegyan, 'Perestroika', op. cit., p. 172).

32. V. Sherbakov, of the Gosstrud, *Lit. Gaz.*, 3 June 1987

33. *Moscow News*, no. 31, 2 Aug. 1987.

34. According to the director of the Institute for the Economies of the Socialist Countries, Bogomolov, inflation in the USSR is running at about 3 to 4 per cent a year (*L'Expansion*, no. 317, Oct. 1987).

35. Farm output rose by 1.2 per cent per year between 1980 and 1985, and by 5 per cent in 1986.

36. Gorbachev, *Kommunist*, no. 10, 1986, p. 6. This form of organization achieved spectacular results at Akshi in Kazakhstan in the 1960s, but its promoter, Khudenko, was condemned and died in prison (*Lit. Gaz.*, 21 May 1969). He was subsequently rehabilitated, but the local authorities appear to be in no hurry to revive the experiment) *Lit. Gaz.*, 1 Apr. 1987).

37. Gorbachev, *Pravda*, 15 July 1987.

38. The text of the bill was published in *Ekonomicheskaya Gazeta*, no. 3, 1988.

39. Repairs to cars, household articles, and garments; carpentry; manufacture and sale of garments, woolens, shoes, furniture, and carpets; taxi services, hairdressing, photography, housework, secretarial work, private tuition, translation, medical consultations, taking in tourists. Local authorities have broad powers to regulate these activities (A. Aganbegyan, 'Perestroika', op. cit., p. 146). The following remain prohibited: the production or

repair of weapons, of precious metals and non-metallic materials, of printing or mimeo machines, of disks, medications, narcotics, cosmetics, candles, icons, or electronic appliances, the organization of video or film shows (statute of 3 May 1976 of the Council of Ministers of the USSR).

40. Four thousand applications were submitted in Kiev on 1 May 1987; some thirty or so private taxis were counted in Tallinn (*Lit. Gaz.*, 7 Jan. 1987); there were twenty-four co-operative restaurants in Moscow (*Moscow News*, 2 Aug. 1987).

41. *Lit. Gaz.*, 18 Feb. 1987.

42. T. Zaslavskaya, *Kommunist*, no. 14, Sept. 1986. By way of illustration, a kilo of potatoes cost ten kopeks in Moscow (July 1987) at the official rate, and 55 kopeks on the kolkhoz markets in provincial towns (*Soc. issl.*, no. 5, 1987, p. 131).

43. Dzokaeva, *Lit. Gaz.*, 3 June 1987. This applies to the simultaneous retention in official documents of the imposed price and free contractual prices, for wholesale and Gossnab supplies. A. Aganbegyan points out that wholesale should come to account for 60 per cent by 1990, and 80–90 per cent in 1992 (Aganbegyan, 'Perestroika', p. 151).

44. Gorbachev, *Pravda*, 15 July 1987.

45. According to S. Bunich, there was only one self-financing enterprise in June 1987, that is, capable of paying its wages out of its own revenues; all other enterprises are financed out of a budget while Gosplan sets their profits, etc. Certain factory managers (e.g. ZIL) receive up to 1,760 planned indicators. (*Lit. Gaz.*, 3 June 1987.)

46. Gorbachev, 26 June 1987 plenum.

47. Gorbachev, 27 June 1987 plenum.

48. Gorbachev, *Pravda*, 15 July 1987.

CHAPTER 3: SOVIET SOCIETY AND CHANGE

1. *Soc. issl.*, no. 1, 1988, p. 121.

2. *Lit. Gaz.*, 12 Sept. 1987.

3. *Pravda*, 15 June 1987.

4. In the fall of 1987, a kilo of tomatoes was selling for 2 rubles in the Moscow markets, which is double the price in the stores; a kilo of beef cost 8–10 rubles, against a state price of 2 rubles. 'The market is for the fat cats,' commented one consumer forced to stand in line outside a store (A. Jacob, *Le Monde*, 31 Oct. 1987).

5. *Pravda*, 15 July 1987.
6. Popov, *Lit. Gaz.*, 4 Mar. 1987
7. *Masovaya informatsiya v sovetskom promyshlennom gorode*, 1980, pp. 245–46.
8. *Le Point*, 2 Nov. 1987, telephone survey of 1,000 anonymous correspondents.
9. Survey conducted in 1985 of a sample of one thousand people (Anarishenko, *Lit. Gaz.*, 8 Oct. 1986).
10. L. Velikanova (*Lit. Gaz.*, 7 Oct. 1987) has revealed that Gosplan is obliged to wait until the next census, in 1989, in order to work out how many new apartments need to be built, because until now its calculations had been based on floor space and not on numbers of apartments.
11. *Leningradskii rabochii*, 18 Apr. 1986.
12. There are 129,000 living in the steel industry's hostels, and twice as many in those of the textile industry. According to a survey of these hostels, 20 per cent of a young worker's budget (16 per cent for a woman) is spent on drink (*Eko*, no. 11, 1985, p. 150). In certain towns, young people have been given permission to put up a co-operative building of their own, but members are selected on the basis of their performance in socialist-emulation campaigns.
13. In Vologda, pop. 273,000, 'We haven't seen butter for years' (*Lit. Gaz.*, 29 Apr. 1987, p. 10).
14. Sales are authorized between 2 and 7 P.M. (instead of 11 A.M. to 8 P.M.).
15. The line is so long that people taking the Moscow subway to the Gastronom are advised to alight one stop early.
16. The ration was two bottles per month per person aged over 20.
17. 'The fall in alcohol consumption has reached a point of diminishing returns as it starts to run counter to popular feeling' (*Moscow News*, 5 Aug. 1987).
18. *Soc. issl.*, no. 1, 1986, pp. 43–47.
19. Leonid Abalkin, *Moscow News*, 6 Sept. 1987. For a kilo of beef that retails for 1.80 rubles, the state pays 3 rubles (A. Aganbegyan, 'Perestroika', op. cit., p. 200).
20. Sergei Kiselev, *Lit. Gaz.*, 25 Feb. 1987; L. Nemenova, *Lit. Gaz.*, 30 July 1987.
21. A. Aganbegyan, *Time*, 27 July 1987.
22. N. Ryzhkov, chairman of the Council of Ministers of the USSR, in a statement to the Supreme Soviet on 29 June 1986.
23. Collective letter written by 400 wives of laid-off railroad workers

(*Lit. Gaz.*, 11 Mar. 1986). Tass, 26 Mar. 1987, announced the closing of an enterprise in Leningrad and the firing of two thousand workers. The public also complains that staff cuts in the mail and telephone services are affecting rural populations (*Lit. Gaz.*, 12 Aug. 1987).

24. A Soviet economist's estimate, reported by C. Bohlen, *Washington Post*, 17 Aug. 1987.

25. *Sovetskaya Kultura*, 4 Jan. 1986.

26. *Kommunist*, no. 13, 1986.

27. A 120-bed homeopathic clinic has opened, and at Polyclinic No. 3, a consultation fee of 6.50 to 8 rubles has been instituted, in an effort to make the hospital self-financing. Currently, it is estimated that 19 per cent of patients go to fee-paying clinics. (*Moscow News*, 28 Feb. 1988.)

28. A survey of workers in 141 enterprises in the Urals revealed that 45–60 per cent of them had no opinion about the economic reform (*Izvestia*, 4 Sept. 1987).

29. *Moscow News*, 13 Sept. 1987.

30. The German women's magazine *Burda Moden* proposes to satisfy this curiosity by launching a Russian edition, an innovation ascribed to the influence of Raisa Gorbacheva. This Russian-language version is currently being printed in Germany with a run of 150,000 copies, pending an anticipated growth in circulation to 1.5–2 million, which would justify building a printing press in the USSR.

31. *Lit. Gaz.*, 5 Aug. 1987.

32. Too many Saturdays are given over to 'voluntary' (i.e. compulsory, according to one worker, L. Kibireva) labour, which deprives women of rest and time that could otherwise be devoted to their family (*Lit. Gaz.*, 4 Mar. 1987).

33. Gorbachev's speech given in Minsk, 10 July 1985.

34. *Pravda*, 18 June 1987.

35. *Pravda*, 2 Oct. 1986.

36. Central Committee plenum, January 1987.

37. *Pravda*, 27 July 1986.

38. *Pravda*, 15 July 1986. The term sabotage also crops up in an article by M. Ulyanov, *Kommunist*, no. 5, March 1987.

39. Speech at the Smolny Institute, 13 Oct. 1987.

40. On 10 September, Chebrikov, the head of the KGB, hinted that glasnost was not supposed to serve the subversive ends of enemies 'who are urging certain members of the intelligentsia to criticize, to engage in demagogy and nihilism,' and a few days

later, Ligachev gave a warning to newspaper and magazine editors who might be tempted to publish whatever they pleased (16 July 1987). In a speech given at the Elektrostal factory near Moscow, Ligachev stressed the positive accomplishments of the 1930s, such as collectivization and industrialization.

41. In Kirghizia, the elimination of Turdakun Usubalyev led to the purge of 82 per cent of Party members; in Turkmenistan only 67 of 153 Central Committee members were confirmed in their posts. In Uzbekistan, 200 leaders and 70 per cent of kolkhoz chairmen and sovkhoz managers have been arraigned.

42. V. Drozd, *Lit. Gaz.*, 30 Sept. 1987.

43. A. Strelyany, *Lit. Gaz.*, 28 May 1986.

44. *Pravda*, 3 Feb. 1987.

45. Abel Aganbegyan, quoted in *Le Monde*, 31 Oct. 1987.

46. *Pravda*, 23 Nov. 1985; *Sovetskaya Industriya*, 11 Nov. 1987.

47. *Moscow News*, 6 Sept. 1987.

48. N. Shmelev, *Novy Mir*, no. 6, 1987, pp. 142–48.

49. Statement by the minister of finance, *Pravda*, 20 Aug. 1987.

50. *Lit. Gaz.*, 29 Jan. 1986.

51. G. Breslauer, *Soviet Studies*, January 1984, and *Slavic Review*, vol. 45, Winter 1986.

52. Popov, *Lit. Gaz.*, 4 Mar. 1987.

53. Vladimir Karpov, the new secretary of the Writers' Union, *Lit. Gaz.*, 6 May 1987.

54. For example, the reappearance of the writer D. Granin, who had been banned for having supported Solzhenitsyn's protests over censorship at the fourth writers' congress in 1967 (*Lit. Gaz.*, 18 June 1986), or the publication in *Novy Mir* (no. 6, 1986) of G. Aitmatov's short story 'Plakha' ('The executioner's block'), which deals with the hitherto taboo subject of drugs.

55. The film takes place in Georgia and portrays a caricature of a dictator who resembles a mixture of Beria, Stalin, and Mussolini, while alluding to the ordeals of the population and present-day vestiges of this kind of mentality.

56. At a conference held in Paris in June of 1987, S. Zalygin, director of *Novy Mir*, did not rule out the possibility of publishing the works of Solzhenitsyn if he agreed.

57. *Pravda*, 21 May 1985.

58. Belov has been criticized for tackling a taboo subject when raising the question of Soviet writers who have left the country and relinquished their nationality (*Lit. Gaz.*, 6 May 1987). Similarly, the publication of works by Nabokov in *Moskva* or *Ogonek*, and

the forthcoming publication of his writings in *Novy Mir*, have aroused hostile reactions (*Lit. Gaz.*, 30 Sept. 1987). The works of Joseph Brodsky, who shortly afterwards won the Nobel Prize for literature, were refused by the Moscow Book Fair in September 1987. On the other hand, official homage to Marc Chagall, who left Russia in 1922, was paid in the form of an exhibition of his works at the Pushkin Museum in Moscow.

59. *Novy Mir*, no. 1, 1988.

60. Socialist realism was sharply criticized by the writer Yuri Bondarev at this congress.

61. *Pravda*, 15 July 1987.

62. Speech by Zalygin in Paris, June 1987.

63. The two co-operative publishing houses are Kupar (in Tallinn) and Zharki (in Novosibirsk). The Moscow writers too have been thinking of setting up a co-operative publishing house of their own, but official publishers fear they might lose their best authors if they were to prefer co-operatives prepared to publish more quickly if the state gave them the means (*Lit. Gaz.*, 4 Mar. and 9 July 1987).

64. Speech by Gorbachev to the Congress of Komsomols 15 Apr. 1987.

65. 'They have grown accustomed to hearing lecturers spout truths contradicted by the facts; they have become skeptical' (Boris Olezhnik, *Lit. Gaz.*, 1 July 1987).

66. *Pravda*, 6 Jan. 1987. The police report upward of 130,000 drug addicts notwithstanding the prohibition on poppy-growing in the USSR, but no aggregate figures have been published on prostitution. A survey of Georgia reported 532 women identified as such, one-third of them aged between twenty-one and twenty-five, 53 per cent of them divorced, and two-thirds having been to secondary school. Their prices ranged from 20 to 50 rubles a trick; the chief motivation for young prostitutes is the desire to buy luxury garments, such as a pair of imported boots for 120 rubles (*Soc. issl.*, no. 6, 1987, pp. 58–61).

67. Drugs are entering the USSR via the port of Odessa and Afghanistan (*Lit. Gaz.*, 10 and 24 Dec. 1986). They are also manufactured illicitly in the USSR from poppy plantations – 3,000 hectares were destroyed in 1986 – and Indian hemp – 100,000 hectares destroyed. Four thousand manufacturers have been arrested. The value of these sales for the Republic of Georgia alone is 35.4 million rubles (*Soc. issl.*, no. 1, 1987).

68. A fairly complete list of the fairly informal youth groups (*nefor-*

mal'nye molodezhnye ob'edineniya) is given in I. Sundyev, *Soc. issl.*, no. 5, 1987.

69. *Soc issl.*, no. 7, 1987, pp. 42–43.
70. 'Pered zerkalom: podrostki i dengi', *Lit. Gaz.*, 2 Sept. 1987.
71. From the film *Is It Easy to Be Young?* by Y. Podnieks. The novelist A. Prikhanov also deals with the theme of this war in 'Derovo v centre Kabula' (*Oktyabr*, no. 9, 1986) and in 'Risunki batalista' (*Moskva*, nos. 9 and 10, 1986).
72. *Pravda*, 5 Aug. 1987.
73. A. Lizichev, the general in charge of the Red Army Political Department, *Lit. Gaz.*, 23 Feb. 1987.
74. *Lit. Gaz.*, 13 May 1987.
75. General Gareev (*Lit. Gaz.*, 3 June 1987), who attacks the review *Yunost'* for having published Olga Zhdana's libertarian and anti-militarist novel *Vzroslaya zhizn*. Defense Minister Yazov has attacked the same magazine for having published an article by Writers' Union Secretary Yuri Poliakov, in which he describes the bullying of young recruits by their elders (*stariki*), which does little to enhance the popularity of military service.
76. G. Cicishvili reacted sharply to V. Astafiev, regarding the latter's short story 'Lovlya peskare v Gruzzi' an insult to Georgians (*Lit. Gaz.*, 6 May 1987).
77. Fire at the Tbilisi Opera in 1973, an explosion in the building of the Council of Ministers of Georgia in 1976. Shevardnadze, the minister of the interior, restored order, which earned him promotion to the post of first secretary of the Georgian Party.
78. A. Bak, Chairman of the Soviet of Nationalities of the USSR (*Lit. Gaz.*, 7 Oct. 1987). Interestingly, the Caucasian republics are defending themselves better than the Central Asian Republics against this influx of Russians, since at the last census, the latter represented only 2.3 per cent of the population of Armenia, and 8 per cent in Georgia and Azerbaijan.
79. *Lit. Gaz.*, 6 May 1987. At the Leningrad conference on the October Revolution and Literature at the beginning of October 1987, O. Gonchar protested against cutbacks in local broadcasts on grounds of internationalism, against the closing of Ukrainian schools, which are still being shut down by the hundreds, and against censorship of history classes (*Lit. Gaz.*, 7 Oct. 1987). He returned to his theme (*Lit Gaz.*, 24 Feb. 1988) with a reference to the abolition of the chairs of Ukrainian literature in six teacher-training institutes, and the more contentious problem of ecological disasters (the building of Chernobyl and the flooding

of tens of thousands of acres of fertile land under the water piled up behind hydroelectric dams, in language reminiscent of Rasputin discussing Matyra). The Uzbek writer Akrum Animov has pointed out that Lenin was hostile to the imposition of Russian as a compulsory language and that 'notwithstanding its importance, he did not expect it to be studied under the [threat of the] stick' (*Lit. Gaz.*, 9 Mar. 1985).

80. S. Kunayev, writers' plenum of 29 April 1987 (*Lit. Gaz.*, 6 May 1987). The Kazakh writer A. Nurpeysov welcomes the opening of new Kazakh-speaking schools and kindergartens – which suggests that this measure had been awaited – but regrets the falling print runs of books in this language (*Lit. Gaz.*, 24 Feb. 1988).

81. He expressed the hope that those who make decisions 'would be capable of understanding the history, the traditions, and psychology of the peoples of the republic' (*Lit. Gaz.*, 6 May 1987).

82. The rector of the University of Tashkent has nonetheless refused to comment on the events (*Lit. Gaz.*, 1 Apr. 1987).

83. Yegor Belyaev, *Lit. Gaz.*, 20 May 1987.

84. As in other Soviet cities, there is a strong Muslim community in Moscow, which holds its meetings in Izmailovo Park.

85. The Ingush and Chechens, also deported and rehabilitated, have been given back their territory.

86. The figure of 5,000 authorizations has been quoted (*CSCE Digest*, Aug. 1987).

87. This would explain why Shcherbitsky has been allowed to stay on in the Politburo, and why the recent purges in the Ukraine have been relatively cautious. Nevertheless, the chairman of the Council of Ministers, A. Lyashko, was sacked in July 1987 for an affair involving illegal arrest.

88. President von Weizsäcker is reported to have obtained a promise to allow 2 million Germans to leave (*Time*, 20 July 1987).

89. Statement by R. Kuznetsov, chairman of the OVIR, on 13 Aug. 1987.

90. The rules have been eased for children of refuseniks in possession of state secrets. These are now allowed to submit a separate emigration application if they are eighteen or over.

91. Writers' plenum, *Lit. Gaz.*, 6 May 1987.

92. The Kazakh literary reviews were obliged to take Russians onto their editorial boards for the sake of 'internationalization' (*Lit. Gaz.*, 20 May 1987).

93. *Pravda*, 2 Sept. 1987.

94. Resolution of the twenty-seventh congress, 1986.

95. After his release from a camp, P. Ayrikyan wrote to Gorbachev

in May 1987 to ask for a referendum on independence in Armenia.

96. *L'Express*, 21 Mar. 1987 (opinion poll conducted in Germany, Spain, the United States, Great Britain, and France).

97. According to Gennady Gerasimov of the MID (May 1987), approximately 700 people are in detention on account of their opinions, but dissident sources give figures of between 1,500 and 2,400.

98. Statement to the foreign press, 15 May 1987.

99. Soviet TV broadcast *Vremya*, 17 June 1987.

100. *Lit. Gaz.*, 7 June 1987. The novel *The Pyramid* by Yuri Arakcheev (*Znamya*, nos. 8 and 9, 1987) describes how a trial is manipulated by the prosecution to obtain the conviction of an innocent person.

101. *Lit. Gaz.*, 4 Mar. 1987.

102. *Lit. Gaz.*, 17 Dec. 1986.

103. *Izvestia*, 11 July 1987. According to Helsinki Watch, cited by *CSCE Digest*, Aug. 1987, approximately 100 dissidents are being held in psychiatric hospitals.

104. E. Hurkey, *Soviet Studies*, Apr. 1982, p. 220.

105. Alexander Zinoviev, *Quinzaine littéraire*, Aug. 1986.

106. M. Pavlova-Silvanskaya, *Lit. Gaz.*, 29 Apr. 1986.

107. S. Pavlov, *Soc. issl.*, no. 4, 1987, p. 39.

108. Ibid., p. 41.

109. C. Kharchev, official in charge of relations with religious groups, *Moscow News*, 26 July 1987.

110. D. Likhachev has drawn attention to this role and claimed that the Orthodox Church is entitled to produce the publications its believers require (*Lit. Gaz.*, 9 Sept. 1987).

111. The Bishop of Vilnius has called upon believers to work conscientiously and display respect and tolerance for others (*Moscow News*, 5 July 1987).

112. *Moscow News*, 4 Oct. 1987.

113. *La Croix* (Paris), 21 Aug. 1987. A. Solzhenitsyn wrote to this same patriarch in 1972.

114. With pronounced regional variations which placed the western regions of the USSR at the top of the league for religious observance: 60 per cent of the population of western Byelorussia attend church regularly; 80 per cent of marriages in Lvov (western Ukraine) are celebrated in church. In 1985, 58 per cent of seminary admissions in Leningrad were Ukrainians (S. Pavlov, *Soc issl.*, no. 4, 1987, p. 42).

115. Ibid., p. 35.

116. Ibid., p. 39.

117. 'Dissidence belongs to the past', Alexander Zinoviev, *Quinzaine littéraire*, Aug. 1987.

CHAPTER 4: THE GREAT DEBATE

1. M. Pavlova-Silvanskaya, *Lit. Gaz.*, 28 Apr. 1978.
2. F. Burlatsky, *Lit. Gaz.*, 16 Apr. 1986.
3. Stalin, *The economic problems of Socialism in the USSR* (1952). N. Voznesensky, chairman of Gosplan until 1949 (executed the following year), advocated a substantial price reform just after the war.
4. Nemshinov, Novogilov.
5. G. Lisichkin, *Plan i Rynok*, 1966.
6. Bonzhursky, roundtable on economic reform, *Lit. Gaz.*, 3 June 1987.
7. *Lit. Gaz.*, 21 Jan. 1987.
8. *Lit. Gaz.*, 3 June 1987.
9. *Lit. Gaz.*, 28 Apr. 1987.
10. *Lit. Gaz.*, 3 June 1987.
11. N. Shmelev, *Novy Mir*, no. 6, 1987.
12. *Lit. Gaz.*, 3 June 1987. E. Stefanovich, by the way, denies that health care is free in the USSR: 'The question as to whether health-care is free or fee-paying does not arise, it has been fee-paying for ages. In Moscow, in all the hospitals I have been to, the only things patients talked about was how much you had to pay and to whom' (*Lit. Gaz.*, 16 Sept. 1987).
13. *Lit. Gaz.*, 3 June 1987.
14. *Lit. Gaz.*, 21 Jan. 1987.
15. G. Lisichkin, *Lit. Gaz.*, 24 June 1987.
16. V. Sherbakov, of Gosstrud, *Lit. Gaz.*, 3 June 1987.
17. G. Batygin, *Soc. issl.*, no. 3, 1987.
18. Self-employed golddiggers can earn 5,000 to 11,000 rubles in a season (F. Abramov, *Nash Sov.*, no. 3, 1986, p. 60).
19. V. Tikhonov and K. Kuzhenikova, *Lit. Gaz.*, 8 Apr. 1987.
20. F. Burlatsky, 'Lenin i strategiya krutogo pereloma', *Lit. Gaz.*, 16 Apr. 1986.
21. F. Burlatsky, *Lit. Gaz.*, 1 Oct. 1986.
22. Stalin taxed the peasants' means of production, not their earnings, which resulted in the uprooting of fruit trees, for example (*Lit. Gaz.*, 8 Apr. 1987).
23. *Soc. issl.*, no. 3, 1987, p. 14.
24. Of those who have any savings at all, 3 per cent have savings in excess of 20,000 rubles. (Gorbat, *Lit. Gaz.*, 15 July 1987.)
25. *Moscow News*, 3 Jan. 1988.

26. Max Weber, *The Protestant Ethic and the Spirit of Capitalism*, 1906.
27. *Lit. Gaz.*, 24 June 1987.
28. *Lit. Gaz.*, 8 Apr. 1987 (stating his opposition to applying the example of Hungary, which has authorized the growth of a private sector, to the USSR).
29. Speech to the third writers' congress (*Lit. Gaz.*, 30 June 1976). N. Rasputin has illustrated this theme in *Proshchanie s Mater'yu* (filmed by Klimov).
30. V. Belov, *Nash Sov.*, no. 7, 1986.
31. Ivan Vasiliev, *Nash Sov.*, no. 12, 1985.
32. V. Belov, 'Vse v peredi', *Nash Sov.*, nos. 7 and 8, 1986.
33. Ivan Vasiliev, *Nash Sov.*, no. 12, 1985.
34. V. Rasputin, *Nash Sov.*, no. 7, 1985.
35. V. Belov, speech to the eighth writers' congress, June 1986.
36. V. Belov, *Nash Sov.*, no. 8, 1986, p. 110; the same theme is found in Bondarev, *Vybor* ('The Choice') 1980.
37. V. Belov, *Nash Sov.*, no. 7, 1986, p. 99.
38. V. Belov, *Nash Sov.*, no. 12, 1985, p. 85.
39. V. Belov, 'Vse v peredi', *Nash Sov.*, nos. 7 and 8, 1986 (one of the characters, Brish, epitomizes the unprincipled, 'cosmopolitan' boorish man).
40. 'O romane Belova', *Nash Sov.*, no. 8, 1987; in another hostile reaction, B. Nikolskii addressed the Leningrad Conference on the Revolution and Literature (*Lit. Gaz.*, 7 Oct. 1987) thus: 'Those who seek inspiration in the Russian *izba* deviate from the ideals of the October Revolution.'
41. S. Zalygin, 'V. Rasputin narodnyi pisatel',' *Lit. Gaz.*, 18 Mar. 1987.
42. Recently, Moscow streets have recovered their former names, and the towns of Brezhnev and Ustinov have gone back to being called Naberezhnye Chelny and Izhevsk.
43. V. Kochetov writing on S. Shurtakov's novel *Odolen* in *Moskva*, nos. 4 and 5, 1986.
44. Roundtable on the theme 'Do we have enough cultivated people?' *Lit. Gaz.*, 13 May 1987. The magazine *Moskva* has indeed begun publication of Karamzin's *History;* on the other hand, the director of the Institute for History, I. Kovalchenko, believes that Klyuchevsky and Soloviev would be unlikely to appeal to a wide public (I. Goldenberg, *Soc. issl.*, no. 6, 1987).
45. D. Granin, *Lit. Gaz.*, 18 Mar. 1987.
46. B. Mozhayev, *Muzhiki i Baby* (*Don* nos. 1 to 3, 1987); D. Granin, *Zubr*, (*Novy Mir*, nos. 1 and 2, 1987).
47. *Pravda*, 9 Aug. 1987; *Ogonek*, Oct. 1987. The latter was quoted

in *Le Monde*, 7 Oct. 1987: 'With four exceptions, all the members of the first Soviet government and of the two pre-1917 Party Central Committees died in the Stalin purges. One hundred thirty-nine members of the Central Committee elected at the seventeenth congress in 1934 also perished.' Attempts to study the history of the interwar period objectively did not start only with glasnost. One would have to survey the historiography of recent years, notably V. Danilov's contributions on the agrarian history of the USSR, including a history of collectivization completed in 1961 that has only now been approved for publication.

48. Gorbachev, speaking to press officials: 'We must never forgive nor justify what happened in 1937–38' (*Pravda*, 15 July 1987). Conversely, Ligachev spoke of the benefits of that period: industrialization and collectivization (Elektrostal speech on 26 Aug. 1987).

49. A USSR Supreme Court decision of 4 Feb 1988 overturned the verdict of the 1938 trial in which N. Bukharin, A. Rykov (a former prime minister), K. Rakovsky, V. Maksimov-Dikovksy, and P. Krugov were condemned.

50. Gorbachev, speech given on 2 Nov. 1987 to mark the seventieth anniversary of the October Revolution.

51. This interpretation does not fit the facts, for 'the kulak as exploiter had been eliminated during the civil war. . . . There were no longer any kulaks at the time of collectivization' (*Lit. Gaz.*, 8 Apr. 1987).

52. A decree of 16 June 1987 rehabilitated a group of very distinguished economists (N. Kondratiev, A. Chayanov, etc.) who had fallen victim to Stalin (*Moscow News*, no. 33, 1987). Assessments of Khrushchev's personality are more balanced. He is credited with de-Stalinization, a revival of agriculture, and efforts to establish military parity with the United States (F. Burlatsky, *Lit. Gaz.*, 24 Feb. 1988).

53. *Pravda*, 15 May 1987. In this speech, Gorbachev expresses concern that 'certain people are seeking revenge through glasnost.' D. Granin had called for justice for the victims of purges (*Lit. Gaz.*, 27 May 1987).

54. J. Polyakov refers to the demographics of World War II: losses totaled 26 million if one includes the fall in the birthrate during the war and 'not including the cost of the 1930s, which has never been ascertained' (*Lit. Gaz.*, 30 Sept. 1987).

55. Kamil Ikramov regrets that school textbooks make no mention of the Russian imperial yoke that the non-Russian peoples had to bear (*Lit. Gaz.*, 7 Oct. 1987).

56. V. Rosliakov, *Lit. Gaz.*, 19 Nov. 1986.

57. *Pravda,* 3 January 1988.
58. D. Granin, *Lit. Gaz.,* 18 Mar. 1987.
59. G. Batygin, *Soc. issl.,* no. 2, 1987, p. 32.
60. V. Rasputin, *Pozhar,* op. cit., p. 23.
61. I. Vasiliev, *Nash Sov.,* no. 12, 1985, p. 32.
62. *Lit. Gaz.,* 13 May 1987.
63. Public opinion is hostile to these special schools and has called for closing them (M. Moskvin, *Lit. Gaz.,* 8 April 1987): 'Cars drive the happy few up to the school gates. They are dressed pretentiously and are ill-behaved. People say they got there by "pulling telephone wires" [*pozvonochniki*] because it was a telephone recommendation that got them admitted.'
64. This would be a fee-paying school (50 rubles per month), because it is run along co-operative lines, but the budget would be under the control of the Finance Ministry, and it would organize all the usual Komsomol activities and preparation for military service as elsewhere (*Lit. Gaz.,* 15 July 1987).
65. V. Rozov, *Lit. Gaz.,* 22 Oct. 1986. Similarly, 'man should be able to find what he needs within himself. . . . No dogma can ever produce this result unless he becomes inwardly aware of this,' says Sviatoslav Rerikh, son of a painter who has drawn his inspiration from Tibet (*Lit. Gaz.,* 3 July 1987) and who now has a following (*Soc. issl.,* no. 5, 1987, p. 60).
66. I. Vasiliev, *Lit. Gaz.,* 28 Jan. 1987.
67. V. Belov, *Nash Sov.,* no. 8, 1986, p. 85; I. Vasiliev, *Nash Sov.,* no. 12, 1985, p. 15.
68. D. S. Likhachev, 'Trivogi sovesti', *Lit. Gaz.,* 1 Jan. 1987.
69. D. Granin, 'O miloserdii', *Lit. Gaz.,* 18 Mar. 1987; and *Lit. Gaz.,* 27 May 1987.
70. D. S. Likhachev, *Lit. Gaz.,* 9 Sept. 1987.
71. 'We don't want to hear about the writer's obligations towards society; he has but one obligation, and that is to tell the truth about the past and present situation in our country' (Y. Pompeev, *Lit. Gaz.,* 1 Oct. 1987).
72. *Soc. issl.* no. 3, 1987.
73. D. Granin, *Lit. Gaz.,* 27 May 1987.
74. Vassily Bykov, *Lit. Gaz.,* no. 23, 14 May 1986.
75. D. S. Likhachev, *Lit. Gaz.,* 9 Sept. 1987.
76. Abuladze's film *Repentance* ends with a question 'on the path that leads to the temple'.
77. In a letter to *Ogonek* denouncing 'petty bourgeois bigotry' (*meshchanskoe khanzhestvo*) of show-business stars, one of today's leading idols, Ala Pugacheva, replies with some ironical remarks on 'state patriotism' (*kazennyi patriotizm*) of those who defend mo-

rality. Andrei Voznesensky has defended the rockers before the writers' plenum, warning listeners about the dangers of misleading generalizations about youth violence, and stressing their responsible attitude over the Chernobyl disaster.
78. Yuri Mushketif, first secretary of the Writers' Union of the Ukraine, *Lit. Gaz.*, 1987.
79. *Moscow News*, 31 Aug. 1987.
80. General Volkogonov, *Lit. Gaz.*, 7 Oct. 1987.
81. Gorbachev, speech given at Murmansk, October 1987.

CHAPTER 5: PERSPECTIVES AND SOCIAL CHANGE

1. 'We have been obliged to acknowledge that we cannot go as fast as we would like. All policies need to be given time to demonstrate that they are well-founded, and if the results fail to materialize, does that mean we were wrong from the start? Does it mean we should go back to sugarcoating reality? Impatience will bring us the opposite of what we were looking for: the return of the conservatives.' (Pavlova-Silvanskaya, *Lit. Gaz.*, 29 Apr. 1987.)
2. 'Working according to the new methods entails risk-taking and honest emulation; which is why it is in the official's interest to crush all that is new' (V. Dudintsev, *Lit. Gaz.*, 25 Mar. 1987).
3. 'Safety first: the dynamic elements of a society will always be in the minority. In the name of security, we believed in socialism.' (G. Lisichkin, *Lit. Gaz.*, 24 July 1987.)
4. Murray Feshbach, *The Soviet Economy: A New Course?* (Brussels: NATO, 1987), p. 117.
5. Moscow: *Soc. issl.*, no. 1, 1988, p. 34. Voroshilovgrad: *Ekonomicheskaya Gazeta*, no. 3, 1988. Seven hundred jobs have been axed at the VAZ automobile works in Togliatti (*Moscow News*, 24 Jan. 1988).
6. *Izvestia*, 6 Jan. 1988.
7. *Moscow News*, no. 1, 1988.
8. Question asked by Yeltsin at the 19 Nov. 1987 plenum, which was to remove him from his position as Moscow Party head. On that occasion, he stated that a third of the letters reaching the Gorkom concerned the Afghan war. (*Die Zeit*, no. 5, 1988.)
9. S. Zalygin, N. Rasputin, et al., *Nash Sov.* no. 1, 1987; V. Astafiev, *Tsar Ryba*, 1976.
10. For instance, a demonstration in March 1987 in Leningrad protesting the demolition of the Hotel d'Angleterre, where the poet Yesenin committed suicide in 1925 (*Lit. Gaz.*, 25 March 1987).

'Our youth must be an active youth that thinks beyond the received ideas. I love these groups of young people who defend the monuments of the past.' (D. S. Likhachev, *Lit. Gaz.*, 20 May 1987.)

11. Similar problems – at Lake Sevan in Armenia, Lake Ladoga, and the Sea of Azov – have aroused the reactions of the intelligentsia (*Lit. Gaz.*, 12 Aug. 1987).

12. *Ogonek*, Sept. 1987.

13. In the Ukraine, where forty-one nuclear reactors have been installed, the population is anxious about the millions of tons of radioactive waste (*Lit. Gaz.*, 1 July 1987).

14. In his science-fiction novel *The Day Lasts More than a Hundred Years*, Chinghiz Aitmatov writes of American and Soviet astronauts who discover a planet without wars or arms.

15. *Komsomol'skaya Pravda* denounced Pamyat as 'an unscrupulous clique inspired by mysticism and Leninism' (quoted in *Time*, 15 June 1987).

16. 'The Russian Idea' inspires those who are hostile to Soviet aid to Cuba and the countries of the Third World, and who preach isolationism.

17. 'Lenin condemned the Great-Power chauvinism [of Russia] as likely to provoke the nationalism of the little nations' (Kamil Ikramov, *Lit. Gaz.*, 10 June 1987).

18. *Pravda*, 2 Sept. 1987.

19. 18 Feb. 1988 plenum.

20. The non-Russian nationalities now form 20 to 25 per cent of the contingents of the Red army; the proportion will of course increase in coming years. The Constitution of 1987 omitted the articles that had accorded the republics power to maintain national militias. The net growth of the population of the six Muslim republics amounted to some 42 per cent of the total net population growth in the Soviet Union. (Murray Feshbach, *The Soviet Economy*, p. 115.)

21. By 1959, 19 per cent of those born in the 1930s worked at non-manual occupations that needed a professional education; today, 34 per cent of those born in the 1950s are so employed (*Soc. issl.*, no 3, 1986, p. 10).

22. *Lit. Gaz.*, 1 Jan. 1987.

23. *Moscow News*, no. 9, 1988.

24. S. A. Efimorov, *Soc. issl.*, no. 1, 1988, p. 88.

25. V. D. Klyuchevsky, *Kurs russkoy istorii*, vol. 5, Moscow, 1958, pp. 307–8.

CHAPTER 6: SECOND OPINION

1. What is more, official growth figures are based on forged returns, leading to a 25–30 per cent overestimate of the cereal crop (Leonid Ivanov, *Lit. Gaz.*, 11 May 1988).

2. Ivan Vasiliev, *Nash Sov.*, no. 10, 1986, pp. 18–19.

3. Ivan Vasiliev, *Nash Sov.*, no. 6, 1986; J. Pomerantz, *Syntaxis* (Paris), no. 20, 1987, pp. 4–10.

4. M. Gorbachev, speech to the fourth congress of Kolkhozians of the USSR, 23 Mar. 1988.

5. Vladimir Sitnikov, 'Izba zakolochennymi oknami', *Nash Sov.*, no. 3, 1988.

6. *Lit. Gaz.*, 1 June 1988.

7. The Statutory Instrument issued by the Ministry of Finance in April 1986 places heavy taxes on earnings in excess of 250 rubles per month.

8. Tax rates ranged from 65 per cent to 90 per cent for earnings in excess of 700 rubles (N. Shmelev, *Novy Mir*, no. 4, 1988, p. 174).

9. This authorization was not always easy to obtain, as some local authorities refused to exonerate speculators who had grown rich from hitherto illegal – now legal – activities.

10. Alexander Nikitin, *Lit. Gaz.*, 17 Feb. 1988.

11. Nikolai Shmelev, *Novy Mir*, no. 4, 1988, pp. 165–66.

12. Alexander Nikitin, *Lit. Gaz.*, 17 Feb. 1988.

13. Although the official price index has remained unchanged, the press reports that the price of shoes rose 18 per cent and textiles by 12 per cent between 1981 and 1988 (*Lit. Gaz.*, 8 June 1988).

14. *Soc. issl.*, no. 2, 1988, p. 62.

15. According to N. Shmelev, out of a total of 260 billion rubles deposited in 1987, 20 to 30 billion probably represent fraudulent earnings or stolen cash (*Novy Mir*, no. 4, 1988, p. 172).

16. *Soc. issl.*, no. 2, 1988, p. 54.

17. N. Shmelev, *Novy Mir*, no. 4, 1988, p. 162.

18. *Lit. Gaz.*, 11 May 1988.

19. N. Shmelev, *Novy Mir*, no. 4, 1988, p. 163.

20. Ibid.

21. 'Nowhere else are there as many domestics as in our country' (G. Semenov, *Lit. Gaz.*, 18 Nov. 1987).

22. Boris Kurashvili, *Moscow News*, no. 23, 5 June 1988.

23. 120 million Soviet citizens earn less than 100 rubles per month (A. Matylev and Orlov, *Lit. Gaz.*, 8 June 1988).

24. *Lit. Gaz.*, 18 May 1988.

25. Alexander Levikov, *Moscow News*, 24 Apr. 1988.

26. The sums on deposit in Soviet savings banks range between 300 and 10,000 rubles (*Soc. issl.*, no. 2,, 1988). Another sign of status is the countless decorations and their different ranks, 'which are every bit as significant as the old regime's celebrated Table of Ranks' (Boris Vasiliev, *Moscow News*, no. 10, 6 Mar. 1988).

27. *Narodnoe khozyastvo SSSR za zolet,* Moscow, 1987, p. 522.

28. *Soc. issl.*, no. 2, 1988, pp. 74–75.

29. *Soc. issl.*, no. 2, 1988, p. 61.

30. Viktor Astafiev, *Lit. Gaz.*, 18 May 1988.

31. *Moscow News*, 29 May 1988.

32. As confirmed by a poll of Muscovites conducted by a French polling firm in early 1988.

33. The agreement provides that Najibullah's Communist government may continue during the nine-month period to receive material assistance in proportion to any aid the Afghan resistance receives from abroad.

34. The Institute for International Relations, the Institute for the Socialist System, and Oriental-affairs specialists.

35. E.g. people like A. Prokhanov, a publicist for the Afghan war, who waxed lyrical over the latest military techniques and attacked the pacifists for hindering the general staff ('Defensive consciousness and new attitudes', *Literaturnaya Rossiya*, 4 May 1988).

36. Vyacheslav Kondratiev, Sashka (Druzhba Narodov) in *Soviet Literature*, no. 7, 1980.

37. *Moscow News*, no. 23, 5 June 1988.

38. Sergei Sukharev, *Lit. Gaz.*, 4 May 1988.

39. *Pravda*, 27 May 1988.

40. The West German and U.S. defense ministers have held discussions to review recent progress made by the USSR in this sphere (F.A.Z., 23 June 1988).

41. I am indebted to the eminent Orientalist, the late Alexandre Bennigsen, for bringing this point to my notice.

42. On 28 Apr. 1988, Soviet TV broadcast a program about an exhibition of treasures collected by leading figures in Uzbekistan.

43. *Lit. Gaz.*, 4 May 1988.

44. The Tadzhiks of Uzbekistan have no schools in their national language, and the Uzbeks in Kazakhstan are in the same situation (T. Pulatov, *Moscow News*, 3 Apr. 1988).

45. The Bashkir Republic publishing house is allowed to publish only two works per year (*Lit. Gaz.*, 4 May 1988).

46. A. Ibramov (Kirghizia), *Lit. Gaz.*, 4 May 1988.

47. Local populations did not learn the level of radiation in Kiev, Chernigov, and Zhitomir until two years after the Chernobyl disaster (*Lit. Gaz.*, 18 May 1988).

48. Timur Pulatov, *Moscow News*, 3 Apr. 1988.

49. K. Ikramov (Uzbekistan), *Lit. Gaz.*, 4 May 1988.

50. Timur Pulatov, *Moscow News*, 12 Apr. 1988.

51. Nearly a thousand Tatars demonstrated in Tashkent on 26 June, and on 28 June, the opening day of the Party conference, 150 Tatars demonstrated in Moscow (Agence France Presse, 28 June 1988).

52. *Pravda*, 10 and 23 June 1988.

53. The Uzbeks are demanding certain parts of Kazakhstan, while the Tadzhiks think that certain towns in Uzbekistan ought to belong to them (Timur Pulatov, *Moscow News*, 12 June 1988).

54. N. Shmelev, *Novy Mir*, no. 4, 1988, p. 161.

55. J. Zasursky (dean of the Moscow Institute of Journalism), *Lit. Gaz.*, 1 June 1988.

56. Anatoly Strelyany (Amsterdam University Symposium, session held on 31 May 1988).

57. N. Shmelev, *Novy Mir*, no. 4, 1988, p. 103.

58. It is planned to cut the number of ministries to around twenty (Kurashvili, *Moscow News*, 5 June 1988).

59. *Sovetskaya Rossiya*, 4 Oct. 1987.

60. The memoirs of Svetlana Alliluyeva, Stalin's daughter, clearly reflect that intellectual's determination to put some distance between herself and the world of politics (*Only One Year*, Harper & Row, 1969).

61. The writer Sergei Zalygin, now chief editor of *Novy Mir*, was the instigator of this campaign, which succeeded, among other things, in safeguarding oil and gas deposits that would otherwise have vanished under water (*Nash Sov.*, no. 1, 1987).

62. Valentin Rasputin, that other apostle of the Siberian ecology, remains concerned for the future of Lake Baikal, reassuring official statements notwithstanding (ibid.).

63. The possibility of republishing these philosophers was raised by A. Losev's report to a recent seminar presented to the Maxim Gorky Institute for World Literature (June 1988).

64. B. Ilizarov, 'Komu vygodny tainy?' (Who benefits from secrets?), *Lit. Gaz.*, 1 June 1988. This source adds that, even among those of the State Historical Archives that are open to the public, 2.4 million are accessible out of a total of 20 million.

65. Notably P. Fedoseyev, vice-president of the Academy of Sciences of the USSR and head of all human sciences, and Kas'junenko, editor of the review *Voprosy istorii* (Questions of History). Both believe in the so-called laws of history so dear to Marxists (cf. the Seminar on 'History and Literature', 27 and 28 Apr. 1988, *Lit. Gaz.*, 18 May 1988).

66. *Moscow News*, no. 24, 12 June 1988.

67. Ibid.

68. *Lit. Gaz.*, 1 Dec. 1988.

69. V. Kozhinov, Pravda i istina, *Nash Sov.*, no. 4, 1988, pp. 160–75.

70. Fedor Burlatsky, 'What kind of socialism do we need?' *Lit. Gaz.*, 20 Apr. 1988.

71. Boris Mozhayev, *Moscow News*, no. 23, 5 June 1988.

72. Chinghiz Aitmatov, 'Plakha' (The Executioner); Tendryakov, *Novy Mir*, no. 4, 1987.

73. Anatoly Strelyany at the University of Amsterdam Symposium, 30 May 1988.

74. Valentin Rasputin in an interview with the Swiss weekly *Die Weltwoche*, 23 June 1988.

75. *Lit. Gaz.*, 1 June 1988.

76. 'Living according to one's conscience means being a spiritual personality whose acts are in accord with the meaning ascribed to man by the generations past', V. Rasputin, *Lit. Gaz.*, 1 Jan. 1988.

77. 'Where are the blackshirts taking us?' *Moskovskaya Pravda*, 30 Jan. 1988.

78. Kornayev (*Lit. Gaz.*, 9 Mar. 1988), V. Rasputin (*Nash Sov.*, no. 2, 1988).

79. It is well known that the former secretary of the Moscow obkom, Boris Yeltsin, met members of Pamyat in May 1987.

80. *Narodnost'* has replaced the utopia of a classless society (Tatyana Gluchkova, *Lit. Gaz.*, 23 Mar. 1988). Under the Nazis, people spoke of the threat that cosmopolitanism posed to Germanic *Kultur*.

81. In 1987, three thousand complaints were lodged with the Council for Religious Affairs and fifteen thousand with the courts.

82. In Leningrad, this work will form part of the activities of the newly formed charitable organization O Miloserdii (compassion), whose chairman is the writer D. Granin and which acts as an umbrella organization for fourteen philanthropic bodies.

83. *Moscow News*, no. 22, 1988.

84. Serge Schmemann, 'Gorbachev enlists Church in Campaign', *International Herald Tribune*, 17 June 1988.

85. Tass, 4 June 1988.
86. On the occasion of the thousandth anniversary, the Roman Catholic Church, notably through Vatican Secretary of State Cardinal Casaroli, who was present at the ceremonies, sought to apply for the restoration of the Uniate Ukrainian Church (although Oriental in rite, it is attached to Rome), which had been forced by a pseudo Council of Lvov to merge with the Russian Orthodox Church. A conference is due to be held on this subject in Finland, with representatives of both Churches attending. Andrei Sakharov has appointed himself spokesman for the demands of the clandestine Uniate Church. But the talks are unlikely to prove successful. The Orthodox Church holds that the Uniate Church was born under pressure exerted by Poland in 1596, when the Ukraine was under its domination, and Gorbachev would be reluctant to allow an autonomous church to stir up nationalist feeling in the Ukraine.
87. This document was published in *La Croix* (Paris), 26 May 1988. The same source adds that there are currently 57 faiths in the USSR, and 15,000 different religious communities or associations, including 6,800 churches open for Orthodox worship.
88. Alex Ogorodnikov, editor of the Christian Community Samizdat, *La Croix* (Paris), 10 June 1988.
89. G. Pomerantz, *Syntaxis* (Paris), 1987, no. 20, pp. 4–10.
90. Yuri Yakovlev, cited in the *Economist*, 2 Apr. 1988.
91. He was so designated by Boris Yeltsin on 30 May 1988, in a widely publicized interview given to a foreign journalist, which he was subsequently forced to deny. Gorbachev, on the other hand, has sought to play down divergences with his counterpart. In a reply to the editor of *Newsweek*, who questioned him on this point, he stated: 'All our leaders, both our political leaders and government leaders, are committed to perestroika and are actively involved in designing and implementing perestroika. . . . It is natural that in the leadership itself there is lively and constant discussion within the framework of perestroika. . . . To present these discussions which are a normal part of the democratic process as division within the leadership would be a great mistake' (*Washington Post Weekly*, 30 May to 5 June 1988).
92. Speech given by Ligachev to the Teachers' Conference, presenting a positive appraisal of Stalinism, *Uchitel'skaya Gazeta*, 27 Aug. 1987.
93. During his twenty-three months at the head of the Moscow Party, Yeltsin replaced fifteen of the eighteen Gorkom secretaries, as

well as the mayor of Moscow, Fedor Promyslov, who had held that post since 1963. Yeltsin was responsible for reopening the national cemetery of Novodivishi, the opening of Izmailovo Park to artists, and the authorization of the conference of perestroika clubs in August 1987.

94. The term *nomenklatura* has become slightly pejorative, so the sociological expression 'leading elites' is now used in its place (N. Moiseyev, 'Oblik rukovoditelia,' *Novy Mir*, no. 4, 1988).

95. Boris Kurashvili, *Moscow News*, no. 25, 5 June 1988.

96. *Pravda*, 27 May 1988.

97. These demands were published in *Sovestkaya Estoniya* on 18 June 1988 (*FAZ*, 23 June 1988) and sparked mass demonstrations in Vilnius to mark the delegates' departure (*FAZ*, 27 June 1988).

98. 'People here know that the Grigoryants "organization" in quotation marks is tied not only organizationally but also financially to the West, that his constant visitors and guests are Western correspondents. Therefore people think of him as some kind of alien phenomenon in our society, sponging on the democratic process, sponging on the positive aspects of perestroika. . . . But we are sure that our country is strong enough to overcome such a thing.' (Gorbachev, *Washington Post Weekly*, May 30, 1988; *Pravda*, 23 May 1988.)

99. Boris Kurashvili, *Moscow News*, 24 Apr. and 5 June 1988.

100. Gorbachev, *Washington Post Weekly*, 30 May 1988; *Pravda*, 23 May 1988.

101. Motilev and Orlov, 'Who should pay for economic fecklessness?' *Lit. Gaz.*, 8 June 1988.

102. N. Moiseyev, *Novy Mir*, no. 4, 1988.

103. Roundtables on judicial reform (*Lit. Gaz.*, 27 Apr. 1988) and the rule of law (8 June 1988).

104. S. E. Deitsevet and I. Shablinski, *Sovestkoe gosudarstvo i Pravo*, no. 7, 1987, pp. 118–20).

105. Sakharov, press conference, 3 June 1988. There are still some 350 political prisoners in the USSR, according to Amnesty International (*Economist*, 4 June 1988).

106. During the first half of 1988, 6,017 Jews (against 8,155 in 1987) and 6,930 Armenians were authorized to emigrate. A larger number of Soviet Germans were allowed to leave – 80,000 in 1987, and an expected 120,000 in 1988.

107. Sakharov's remarks on the KGB are spelled out in a thirteen-page contribution to a collective book prepared by thirty-four

supporters of perestroika recently published in Moscow (*Journal de Genève*, 24 June 1988).

108. Vladimir Melnikov, first secretary of the Autonomous Republic of Komi, who launched this attack and named names at Gorbachev's request, also mentioned G. Afanasiev, editor of *Pravda* since 1968, and Georgi Arbatov, former director of the USA and Canada Institute.

109. 'Women are unable fully to enjoy their rights because they have so many duties to perform and suffer inadequate living conditions and poor child-care facilities. They should be represented on governing bodies at all levels.'

110. Ligachev, protesting that he was not an opponent of perestroika, 'said he had been instrumental in bringing [Yeltsin] into the leadership and that some of his own close relatives had been shot or repressed under Stalin's rule.' (*International Herald Tribune*, 2 July 1988).

111. The president of the Writers' Union, Karpov, gained notice for his misgivings over glasnost. On the other hand Ulyanov, president of the Theatre Workers' Union, scored a great popular success with a speech in favour of Gorbachev.

112. The amendment rejecting the possibility of combining the posts of first secretary with president of the soviet (only 200 nays); the amendment providing that *Pravda* should no longer be the organ of the Central Committee of the Party as a whole (56 ayes).

113. The contents of the six resolutions – concerning the development of perestroika, democratization, the political reforms, glasnost, the reform of the legal system, and inter-ethnic relations – have not been published at the time of writing.

114. N. Shmelev, *Novy Mir*, no. 4, 1988.

115. 'The Council [of the Orthodox Church] is profoundly grateful to you for your benevolence toward the spiritual needs of citizen-believers' (Letter addressed to Gorbachev on June 6, 1988).

116. N. Moiseyev, *Novy Mir*, no. 4, 1988.

117. N. Shmelev, *Novy Mir*, no. 4, 1988.

INDEX

ABOUT THE AUTHOR

■ Basile Kerblay is one of the world's leading experts on Soviet society, and author of *Modern Soviet Society,* which is continued with this volume. He is professor emeritus at the Sorbonne.